ECONOMIC COMMISSION FOR EUROPE

Geneva

DÉPÔT DEPOSIT

Business Incubation

UNITED NATIONS

New York and Geneva, 2001

ECE/TRADE/265

UNITED NATIONS PUBLICATION

Sales No. E.01.II.E.9

ISBN 92-1-116777-9

ISSN 1020-8119

UN2

E/ECE/TRADE/265

LIST OF ABBREVIATIONS

BIC	Business incubation centre
BSC	Business support centre
CIT	Country/countries in transition
EBRD	European Bank for Reconstruction and Development
EU	European Union
FDI	Foreign direct investment
GDP	Gross domestic product
HTP	High technology park
LBAC	Local business assistance centres
OECD	Organisation for Economic Co-operation and Development
R & D	Research and Development
SME	Small and medium-sized enterprise
SPICE	Science Park and Innovation Centre Expert Group (Spice Group)
USAID	United States Agency for International Development
UNDP	United Nations Development Programme

FOREWORD

How can Governments most effectively contribute to creating an enterprise culture? This question lies at the heart of the transition process from a command to a market economy. Today, more than ten years after the fall of the Berlin Wall, one can clearly see that there are no quick fixes for creating a competitive environment conducive to enterprise development.

The United Nations Economic Commission for Europe (UN/ECE) launched its industry and enterprise development programme in the late 1990s to provide a supportive forum where Governments could exchange experiences and learn from each other how to structure public - private sector dialogues in cost-effective ways. The UN/ECE itself has successfully supported public - private sector interfaces in many diverse aspects of trade, investment, transport and energy networks, environmental conservation and industrial cooperation. Using tried and tested methodologies, the UN/ECE's Working Party on Industry and Enterprise Development has initiated a number of programmes to expand the cooperation of the member States regarding entrepreneurship and defining the practices and institutions which seem most cost-effective in stimulating an entrepreneurial environment.

The second edition of this publication is one of the first results of the new Enterprise Development Programme. These Guidelines on Best Practice in Business Incubation present some of the lessons learned to date in the countries in economic transition. They illustrate the status of local institutions set up to foster entrepreneurship and encourage growth and competitiveness among small and medium-sized enterprises (SMEs). The main focus is on science parks and business incubators in central and eastern Europe and the Commonwealth of Independent States.

The UN/ECE Team of Specialists on Business Incubation has brought together a wide range of experience from its member States. One of its goals is to assist in developing networks of science parks, technopoles and business incubators to encourage exchanges of practical experience. The Guidelines demonstrate the large variety of models selected by Governments throughout the region. The efforts to build capacity to encourage enterprise development take many forms, and the process is still evolving. "Best practice" is not a static concept – there is still much need for improvement. No definitive models yet exist which provide convincing templates for institution building. But just as each national culture varies, so, too, do the responses to the challenges of creating conditions favourable to market economies and entrepreneurship.

Twenty-seven countries, and the European Commission, participated in the networking, which led to the update of the Guidelines. We hope that the countries will continue to work with each other and exchange experiences on an ongoing basis. At the UN/ECE, we shall continue to contribute to these common goals with a future programme of guidelines in related areas, to foster trade, investment and enterprise development.

Danuta Hübner

Executive Secretary, United Nations Economic Commission for Europe

United Nations Under-Secretary-General

ACKNOWLEDGEMENTS

The UN/ECE secretariat wishes to thank the following individuals and organizations for their valuable contributions to this book:

Mr. Olavi Änkö, Finland; Ms. Olga Apatenko, Ukraine; Mr. Csaba Babos, Hungary; Mr. Gheorghe Bala, Romania; Ms. Staša Baloh-Plahutnik, Slovenia; Mr. Gabor Bierer, Hungary; Mr. Laszlo Bözöményi, Hungary; Mr. Zdenek Broz,Czech Republic; Mr. Laszlo Budavari,Hungary; Mr. Constantin Bulgac,Republic of Moldova; Dr.Hans-Joachim Burghardt, Germany; † Mr. Jiří Coupek, Czech Republic; Mr. Antal Csiszar, Hungary; Mr. Jiri Danes, Czech Republic; Ms. Ludmila Dicum, Moldova; Ms. Petya Drakalieva, Bulgaria; Mr. Enn Erme, Director, Estonia; Ms. Annie Favrie, France; Mr. Heinz Fiedler, Germany; Ms. Necla Haliloglu, Turkey; Mr. Adriana Hangany, Romania; Mr. Gavorg Hachatryan, Armenia; Mr. Jozef Hosmaj, Slovakia; Ms. Liudmila Istomina, Belarus; Mr. Darko Jardas, Croatia; Mr. Sten Johansson, Sweden; Mr. Veniamin Kaganov,Russian Federation; Ms. Katarina Kellenbergerova, Slovakia; Mr. Saidmurod Khairidinov, Tajikistan; Mr. Teimuraz Kortua, Georgia; Ms. Emilia Koupenkova-Radeva, Bulgaria; Mr. Istvàn Kovàcs, Hungary; Ms. Vjera Krstelj, Croatia; Mr. Polad Kuliyev, Kazakhstan; Mr. Krzysztof Kwatera, Poland; Mr. Iztok Lesjak, Slovenia; Mr. Paul Lewis, United Kingdom; Ms. Tatyana Lukyanova, Russian Federation; Mr. Dzintars Lukjanskis, Latvia; Mr. Sergej Miloshevski, the Former Yugoslav Republic of Macedonia; Professor Fabian C Monds, United Kingdom; Mr. Valeriu Moscalu, Republic of Moldova; Mr. Zafar Mukhitdinov, Uzbekistan; Mr. Ray Muscat, Malta; Mr. Jiri Navratil, Czech Republic; Mr. Alistair Nolan, OECD; Mr. Tayfun Oner, Turkey; Dr. Gabriele Orlandi, Switzerland; Ms. Darja Osvald, Slovenia ; Ms. Lyubov Panayotova, Bulgaria; Mr. Ivan Pezlar, Director, Slovakia; Mr. Sergey G. Poliakov, Russian Federation; Mr. Dieter Rabensteiner, Austria; Mr. Lubomir Rajdl, Czech Republic; Ms. Signe Ratso, Estonia; Mr. Raffaele Ricciuti, Italy; Mr. Ravil Sabirjanov, Uzbekistan; Mr. Piotr Sadowski, Poland; Mr. Aleksander Sazanov, Belarus; Dr. Duane Shelton, United States of America; Mr. Ivan Shvets, Ukraine; Mr. Vladimir Sidorov, Russian Federation; Mr. Vittorio Simoncelli, Italy; Mr. Edvins Snore, Latvia; Dr. Anikó Soltész, Hungary; Ms. Doris Sošic, Croatia; Ms. Jadranka Švarc, Croatia; Mr. Sergey Tretiakov, Ukraine; Mr. Lubos Vavra, Czech Republic; Dr. Thomas von Waldkirch, Switzerland; Mr. Krzysztof Zasiadly, Poland; Ms. Gabriella Zulauf, Hungary; Ms. Rahilya Zynalova, Azerbaijan.

BACKGROUND

The second edition of the *Guidelines on Best Practice in Business Incubation* aims at presenting the latest experiences and lessons learnt in the UN/ECE network of business incubators, science parks and technopoles. Particular attention is paid to updating the information in transition economies, in order to discuss the methods required for establishing successful business incubation services in central and eastern Europe and the Commonwealth of Independent States.

The first edition was a result of a Team that was established as an outcome of the Expert Meeting on "Best Practice in Business Incubation" in Geneva in June 1999. The Team consists of more than 100 policy makers and experts from 27 countries.

In preparing the second edition, the members of the Team of Specialists re-examined the situation in their respective countries with a view to creating guidelines on the best practical solutions developed for such institutions to operate and commercially utilize their national and local resource base. The ultimate goal of the work is to promote similar activities throughout the transition economies and share the lessons learned among the member States of the UN/ECE.

For further information, please contact Mr Mika Vepsäläinen at the UN/ECE secretariat: E-mail: enterprise@unece.org or by telephone +41 22 9173197 or fax +41 22 9170178.

PART I

FUNDAMENTALS

CHAPTER 1
DEFINITIONS

Incubators are "start-up ventures whose purpose is the development of other start-up companies" (Rice and Matthews).

Business support centres (BSC), incubators and technoparks all try to provide new small and medium-sized enterprises (SMEs) with the resources necessary to improve their chances of success. Different entities emphasize different mixes of space, training, capital, human and computer networking, consulting, etc. Several definitions have been proposed, but definitions have to be flexible to fit current usage. To cover all of these various entities, the term "Local Business Assistance Centres" (LBAC) has been suggested. Generally, business support centres emphasize soft resources such as training, while technoparks emphasize physical resources such as space. The best business incubators try to provide all the resources for small businesses' survival and growth. While technoparks often focus on space and business support centres on consulting, but incubators identify the bottlenecks and try to overcome them. Depending on the environment, the bottleneck could be space, training, access to capital or markets, infrastructure such as computer networks, and many others.

In fact, instead of speaking about "business incubators" emphasis should be put on the term "business incubation" - an interactive development process aiming at encouraging people to start their own businesses and supporting start-up companies in the development of innovative products. Incubation also means the development of a supportive and stimulating environment for entrepreneurship

The main types of institution that offer, among others, business incubation services are as follows:

o Classical business incubators could be a nursery and start-up unit; a community or enterprise workshop. They provide small start-up firms with premises, infrastructure, and a range of services that can improve their ability to initiate and run their operations during the early development period;

o Industrial estates offer a dynamic approach to regional economic development, local municipalities and regional development agencies;

o Export processing zones can be very useful for the development of export and foreign trade potential and, in general, have a better linkage with the international community, although they have shown little potential to strengthen the local economy. However, through facilitating business services, providing access to infrastructure and providing tax incentives, they aim at attracting foreign direct investment. They also generate employment and contribute to improving the balance of payments;

o Science (technology) parks provide a creative environment for attracting and promoting research commercialization, and technology-based enterprises;

o Virtual business incubators (technology parks) make services available in cyberspace. They connect companies with one another, customers, suppliers, partners, as well as the operating management of the virtual incubator through the Internet, electronic data interchange, videoconference capabilities, etc.;

o Clustering and networking During the 1990s clusters and networking have been increasingly important for the development of SMEs. Through clusters and networks, SMEs can access skilled and highly educated labour and pooled business services including business incubation services. Clusters are an agglomeration of SMEs, working in geographic proximity to one another and in the same sector where appropriate clustering of complementary businesses is more efficient and sustainable than business incubators with different single businesses. These opportunities permit specialization, build technological capability, adaptability, innovation, and competitiveness.

The following international organizations have defined business incubators as follows:

European Commission

"A business incubator is a place where newly created firms are concentrated in a limited space. Its aim is to improve the chance of growth and rate of survival of these firms by providing them with a modular building with common facilities (telefax, computing facilities, etc.) as well as with managerial support and back-up services. The main emphasis is on local development and job creation. The technology orientation is often marginal."

United States National Business Incubation Association (USNBIA)

The USNBIA defines the business incubator as "an economic development tool designed to accelerate the growth and success of entrepreneurial companies through an array of business support resources and services. A business incubator's main goal is to produce successful firms that will leave the programme financially viable and free-standing."

The Science Park and Innovation Centre Expert Group (SPICE)

The SPICE Group is a global network of experts in business incubation, innovation centres, technology parks, regional economic development, technology transfer and entrepreneurship from national and international associations of business incubators and technology/science parks in 25 countries. The SPICE Group has defined the business incubator concept as follows:

o A Science/Technology Park is:
- property based in a defined area of and buildings meant for knowledge/ technology based research, development and production facilities
- linked with public institutions of research and education
- managed to support the transfer of technology as well as the establishment and growth of new (innovative) companies

o A Business Incubator/Innovation Centre Offers rooms for lease, start-up consulting and business planning as well as shared office services to (technology based) innovation companies and entrepreneurs. Such a centre aims at promoting local and regional economic development, the transfer

of technology and innovation as well as the creation of jobs. There are different types of incubators, the most typical being:
- Mixed use incubators promoting economic development and growth through enterprise development and offering services to all kinds of enterprise (low-tech, no-tech, light manufacturing, services)
- Economic development incubators focused on specific targets, such as job creation or industrial restructuring. These institutions are often policy driven and heavily managed under local or regional Governments.
- Technology incubators promote technology-based (start-up) companies with a particular view to the transfer and diffusion of technologies. These are often linked to universities, research institutes and or science and technology parks and, thus, focus on specific industrial clusters and technologies.

In some UN/ECE member countries, business incubation is defined as follows:

Azerbaijan

Business incubators are organizations, creating favourable environment for start-up compnies. Incubators offer space for start-ups and provide the necessary managerial, legislative and accounting backup.

Croatia

The goal of business incubators is to help establish larger numbers of innovative small and medium-sized firms. The incubators help new firms to survive in thefirst few years of existence and to grow, until they acquire such strenght and level of competitiveness that they can enter new markets with a clear business concept and strong management. such companies are then released from the ncubator making room for new young companies.

The mission of the technology transfer centres is to utilize the resources of universtities and institutes in the development and revitalization of industry and business. They provide effective support to research and development projects connecting research institutions with industries and SMEs.

Czech Republic

A business and Innovation Centre is a professional organization, which provides small and medium-sized innovative companies with comprehensive services, integrates the entrepreneurial and territorial entitites and contributes to the development of innovative entrepreneurial activities through partnership with local and regional organizations, such as territorial authorities, local chambers, academic and research organizations, financial institutions, entrepreneurial entities, etc.

All business and innovation centres in the country provide innovative companies with basic and specialized consultations and take part in technology transfer and training. They cooperate closely with local and regional authorities and are also involved in a number of national and international programmes.

The centres are regular members of the European Business and Innovation Centre Network in Brussels (EBN) and as a standard for BICs' actitivities, the Vade-mecum prepared by EGN is used, which provides training for the BIC staff and monitors and evaluates the BIC network. The membership also ensures cooperation with some 140 other BICs throughout the Eurpean Unioan and the associated countries, including access to their databases and information.

A science park or science centre, technology park or technology centre, business and innovation centre are the three most common types of institution in the Czech Republic oriented towards science, technology and innovation-based business. They provide the necessary preconditions for the dynamic development of activities of innovative firms. Such institutions promote technological development by increasing the competitiveness of companies in the market through the development of innovative small and medium-sized firms that are flexible carriers of technological progress. This work helps create jobs as part of the Government's employment policy and structural changes within the regions. Science and technology parks have also an important educational role and, in the field of research and development, they are supposed to cooperate with local universtities and other relevant institutions.

Georgia

Incubators are organizations, which create favourable conditions for those who wish to set up a new business in a professional manner. The experienced and skilled specialists in various fields assist new firms to survive in the curial initial stages.

Incubators offer space for enterprises, consultation, acquaint client enterprises with business world, repay interest on loans and offset losses and in this manner give small business-persons an opportunity to gain knowledge and experience and also to acquire a reputation. All these give the opportunity to small businesses to become strong and independent in the future.

Germany

Business incubators in Germany have a history of more than 16 years, as the Berlin Centre for Innovation and New Enterprises, the first business incubator in Germany, started in November 1983. This initiative was develped by the Technical University of Berlin and was based on experience from technology transfer aimed at promoting the cooperation of small and medium-sized enterprises and the university. The most important reasons for establishing the business incubators were:

o promoting the transfer of results from university research into practical use by supporting scientists starting their own enterprise;
o developing the economic structure of the City of Berlin by facilitating the establishment of new and innovative enterprises with new products or services;
o involving the innovative potential of research facilities of the city in regional economic development;
o creating new future-oriented jobs in new companies as well as in existing small and medium-sized enterprises by using the (indirect) innovative impulse of technology and knowledge based start-up firms cooperating with existing companies.

The concept of the first business incubator in Germany has been clearly focused on technology- and knowledge-based companies. However, the principle of business incubators has rapidly been adapted to different backgrounds and purposes.

Meanwhile all different kinds of incubators are operating in Germany - altogether more than 300.

Although not agreed as a valid norm, there are some definitions more or less accepted by most of the business incubation professionals. A global survey carried out in 1996 by the SPICE / ICECE Group compared the definitions for the terms "science park", "technology park" or "business incubator" used in various countries. The definitions summarized from this survey are used by the ADT, German Association of Technology and Business Incubation Centres, as well:

o Science/Technology/Research Park is a property-based project with an area of land (and buildings) assigned for the purpose of the park:
  - the use of the facilities is earmarked (mainly) for knowledge/technology-based research, development and production companies
  - the park management has (formal) links with public institutions of research and/or higher education (universities, polytechnics etc.)
  - the park is managed to support the transfer of technology as well as the establishment and growth of new (innovative) companies.
  - the practical instruments and working patterns used to build up and operate a science/technology park as well as the aims of such projects are different. Therefore every project has to be developed individually, based on local resources and potentials and respecting the legal and social framework. But despite of all differences the concepts of science and technology parks on the other hand have much in common:
  - the property basis: an area of land to be developed under the management of the science/ technology park and used for defined purposed and in a given framework of conditions (e.g. building restrictions, environment protection);
  - the research and development focus: concentration on specific kinds of use. All facilities in the park are focused on research and development as well as education and training. In some cases there are even technology-related focuses, such as biotechnology, telecommunication, computer technologies;
  - the research link: formal collaboration links with universities and/or other research institutions mainly motivated by the aim to secure the flow of information between science and application/ production and create highly qualified jobs in industry. To make this cooperation easier, specific patterns are defined e.g. for the use of university facilities or for the possibilities of university employees to work for/with industry in specific projects;
  - the technology transfer target: Strengthening the transfer of technology between the research institutions and industry (emphasis on small and medium enterprises) is aimed at supporting the innovation process (new products, processes, services) in industry and increasing the quality of education by organizing feedback between the "producers" (university) and the "user" (industry);
  - the incubation function is not necessarily part of a science and technology park concept, but increasingly parks are integrating innovation centres (concentrated on technology-based firms). These centres help to establish new companies based on the use the research results (from universities as well as from industry);
  - the general aim is to develop wealth in the community or region. Depending on the concept, the size and the time of development of the science/technology park, the impact can reach anything from the local to the (inter-)national level.

o Examples for the different approaches for the development of science and technology parks:
  - developing a new science and technology district of a city: WISTA

Berlin;
- an inner city science and technology park (e.g. the Technology Centre Dortmund, the Technology Centre Aachen or the BIG/TIB Berlin).

o Innovation Centre is a collective term used for many other names such as business incubator as well as business, innovation, or technology centres. In general terms the aim of innovation centres is to create wealth for the local/regional community.

Innovation centres are institutions providing the following services:
o start-up advisory (business planning) and company development consulting;
o letting of appropriate office, laboratory and/ or production space;
o technical and organizational services for young (innovative) enterprises (e.g. secretariat, telecommunication, conference facilities);
o innovation and technology-oriented services (technology - transfer) as well as training and information.

This is not a very sophisticated definition, but it is a sufficient, practical one. Depending on the local situation and the defined aims of a specific innovation centre, the balance of these services differs. In other cases services might be added to this list, e.g. joint laboratories or workshops, specialized (international) marketing services access to, databases, training programmes etc. The key for success is to remember that innovation centres are and have to be based on local/regional resources, concentrate on specific goals and cooperate with local/regional institutions.

Increasingly specialization of innovation centres is developing. Focuses are on certain technological fields or business areas. Relatively new is the development of specialization an international companies and/or business cooperation with foreign partners. An example is the East - West - Cooperation - Centre (OWZ).

Hungary

Business incubators are defined in line with the generally agreed international definitions above.

As regards industrial parks, the fundamental principles of the Hungarian Industrial Park

Programme include:
o To support the development of small and medium-sized enterprises;
o To integrate sectoral and regional views of
o To provide the enterprises participating in the subcontracting programme with an opportunity to settle down and operate under favourable conditions;
o To integrate industrial and regional policy since they build on the local initiatives, support them, activate local resources and contribute to employment;
o To provide an organized, transparent environment and conditions for foreign direct investment.

Italy

A business innovation centre (BIC) is part of the incubator and the BIC assists the actual birth of the incubator and also the growth of entrepreneurial initiatives. A BIC's role is tied up with the following phases:

o The feasibility analysis phase to scrutinize the ideas which entrepreneurs present. The objective is an analysis of the enterprise and the feasibility of the idea itself - planning the future, the financial sources, the developing of an operative plan and marketing details. The output of the phase is a Business Plan;

o The incubation phase is the period in which the entrepreneur needs the maximum support in order to optimize the utilization of time and also reduce costs. During this phase the entrepreneur will find it useful to have a physical space at his/her disposal, a space provided with a series of services where the costs are calculated according to the use made of these same services. This is the time the entrepreneur uses to organize a structure and find financing so as to verify the feasibility of the initiative in real terms It is also the time when the risk of failure is highest;

o The start-up phase is the moment in which the entrepreneur starts to operate, the production areas have been singled out and the machinery bought, so the entrepreneur can devote all his/her attention to the organization, production and the sales. As the entrepreneur gradually gains experience, the risk of failure lessens.

The maturity phase is the time during which the business is fully operative and has a stable productive and commercial organization.

Kyrgyzstan

First of all, a business incubator creates a favourable environment for a limited number of enterprise to grow. The most important feature of an incubator is the set time limits for the incubation period. The incubator caters for and serves the companies during the incubation period but may render certain after-care services to companies that have already completed the process and left the incubator. Another important feature is the need for monitoring the financial operations of the client, i.e. the companies are under permanent supporting control of the incubator throughout the incubation period.

Latvia

The basis for the development of innovative business support structures in Latvia such as technology parks and centres was a new concept for the development of technology centres worked out by the Ministry of Education and Science in 1992, i.e. much earlier than the Concept on Innovative Activities. The initiator of the commercialization of scientific results was the Department of Higher Education and Science of that Ministry. The reason was a dramatic decrease in the number of researchers at the institutes of the Academy of Sciences, universities and industrial research institutes owing to a decrease in the financing of research since 1991. According to the concept, the goal of structures such as technology and innovation centres and science and technology parks is to fill the gap between higher education and scientific institutions and industry, as well as to promote economic development through support to small and medium-sized enterprises (SMEs). At the same time, it is very important to promote international economic and scientific collaboration in designing high quality products and creating jobs for highly-qualified specialists and researchers who had lost their jobs as a result of the reorganization of the higher education system in Latvia. Besides, these structures offer advisory services in business planning, marketing, quality management, market research, international

cooperation, etc to the new enterprises. Thus, the technological parks and centres can promote cooperation among scientific research institutions, industrial and trade enterprises meeting the demands of a market economy and facilitating the emerging small private technology-oriented enterprises. The Statute of the LTICA is the first official document, which defines business support structures in Latvia.

The definitions accepted by the LTICA are the following:

o   Business Incubator (BI) is a structure which can offer services and support to every kind of business in every industry branch, such as leasing rooms and providing technical and secretarial services. The basic function of the BI is to assist the start-up of new enterprises and provide them with information on different legislative acts and to offer consultation on marketing, company management, finance, and other aspects of business;

o   Technological (Innovation) Centre (TC) is a structure, which mainly offers services and support to technology-oriented (knowledge-based) enterprises. Basically, a TC has three functions: a) the same as for the business incubator (rooms for lease, technical and secretarial services, telecommunications, etc.); b) special consultation and information to technology-oriented business, a support in the participation in exhibitions and international cooperation, advertising new products, etc.; and c) advisory services for obtaining loans and other kinds of financial support;

o   Technology Transfer Centre (TT) is an organization to promote the development and production of technology-based products through the transfer of knowledge and research results from research institutions and laboratories to industry, including technology-oriented SMEs;

o   Science (Technology) Park (TP) is a plot of land and a complex of several buildings to be used for knowledge/technology based research, development and production. Higher education and research institutes, technological or innovation centres, business incubators, consultant bureaux, service centres, etc. can also be located in a science park. The basic function of a TP is to manage the area and buildings with a view to developing high-tech business efficiently and maintaining permanent links between research laboratories and technology-oriented companies and to promoting the establishment and growth of innovative companies, including joint ventures. Usually a TP is established near a university or research centre. The tenant companies at the TP can often gain certain fiscal and economic privileges;

o   Technopole (TE) is a whole city, or part of it, with a favourable infrastructure and a legal status encouraging the development of technology-based business, i.e. design and production of new technology based products. A TE usually includes a technology and/or industrial park, an innovation centre, several large enterprises and a large number of technology-oriented SMEs.

Republic of Moldova

A Business Incubator is a limited place with a favourable environment for the development of new businesses, ideas and projects. The regulations regarding Business Incubators are being developed and will be adopted by a Decree of Government of Moldova.

Poland

A Business Incubator aims at creating an atmosphere that favours the linking of public means and private capital in order to meet the needs of businesses at critical stages of their development.

Russian Federation

A business incubator is an organization that supports small businesses by creating favorable conditions and providing production, information, financial and other recourses for private entrepreneurs and small enterprises at the early stages of business formation and development.

A business incubator offers to its clients equipped and safe premises at stable rental conditions, access to credit and training, consulting services (in business development, licensing, insurance, registration, patenting and other fields) and other professional services (such as legal, accounting, marketing services etc.). It also protects businesses from having to solve a number of problems related to maintenance of premises, sanitary, fire-safe and labour regulations and some others.

The psychological climate at a business incubator promotes effective work of businesses, partnership affiliation, and stress reduction. A business incubator provides services to a wide range of small enterprises from start-ups to ones that already have some business experience, as well as to business incubator tenants and outside clients.
Thus, the essence of business incubator support to small businesses is in creation of favorable, "greenhouse" conditions for speeded-up business growth, which is achieved by protecting companies (fully or partially) against negative environmental factors, and at the same time, by satisfying needs that arise at different stages of business development.

Slovenia

A technology park is an organization for the support for businesses based on advanced technologies. Judging by experience around the world, technology parks are one of the most effective forms of assisting and promoting the development of businesses based on advanced technologies. They normally form part of the economic and social development strategy of a city, region or country, and provide businesses at the apex of the technological pyramid with support in the form of premises, administration, information, marketing, capital and credibility.

Technology parks provide an environment with favourable conditions for founding and running companies based on technologies or knowledge-intensive products and services. They allow such companies access to up-to-date technological expertise and equipment, provide links between those with the ideas and capital, industry and the market, and offer management and marketing services. Typically they offer proximity to research centres, universities and multinational companies. Around the world science, technology and industrial parks are principally based on land definition and planning initiatives.

Incubators are environments that stimulate growth in knowledge-intensive start-ups and that stimulate entrepreneurial persons with business ideas to found companies based on the idea.

The incubator is very often a part of a Science- or Technology Park, a powerful environment for the type of companies that the incubators are directed at.

Other definitions:

Research parks - environment for research companies and activities with a strong link to universities. The staff actively stimulates growth of the park tenants as well as technology transfer.

Science parks - environment for research and development-focused companies with links to universities. Some production (scale-up or light manufacturing) activities can be found in a Science park. The staff actively stimulate growth of the park tenants as well as technology transfer.

Technology parks - environment for technology-based companies with links to universities. There is more production to be found in a Technology park than in a Science park. The staff actively stimulates growth of the park-tenants as well as technology transfer.

Industrial parks, business parks, office parks and many other types of park are known as traditional industrial areas with a focus on certain kinds of company and with no formal links to universities and no formalized programme designed to support tenant companies.

CHAPTER 2

GUIDING PRINCIPLES

The Expert Meeting of "Best Practices in Business Incubation" provided an extensive picture of the present state of the incubator infrastructure in the UN/ECE region from Sweden to Turkey, and from the United States to Tajikistan. Building on the practical experience of different economies, the following principles were discussed:

o One of the frequent issues of debate in an incubator is how long the incubation period should last. Should it be limited, and if so, what would be the optimal duration of the incubation? Many local business advisory centres receive start-up support for a few years and are then expected to sustain themselves indefinitely. The start-up support should probably go on for at least three to five years for optimal sustainability;

o When developing entrepreneurship both in advanced market economies and countries in transition it is necessary to build on the experience of incubators to encourage new enterprises. There is now sufficient experience with business incubators and how they fit into the process of economic development, and what their core services are. A decision to start a business incubator thus requires careful planning and preparation and should be based on a thorough and objective analysis;

o The members of the management team should represent both the local Government, local private business organizations, community organizations and local educational institutions. This team generally consists of up to 10 people. One person should be designated as the leader;

o The management team has to determine the purpose of the incubator. Business incubators may have a multitude of purposes, among which the following are possibly the most important:
   - job creation;
   - establishment of start-up companies;
   - modernization, transfer of

technology,
- use of new scientific discoveries;
- business incubators can also be created for specific purposes, such as helping women, immigrants, or minorities.

Some further aims can be identified:
- the economic growth of a region;
- the diversification of the region's industry;
- the multiplication of the sponsor's investment;
- the increase of the region's economic activity.

o The team will determine the types of tenant the incubator will house and the conditions for entry. For SMEs the conditions for entry to a business incubator could be the following:
- the entrepreneur should have a conception about his/her future business;
- the entrepreneur should have a business plan;
- the entrepreneur has to be a beginner in his/her business.

o The team has to possess information regarding the employers in the region, the types of business located in the community, general income and earnings, local taxation, the availability of reasonably priced office space, leasing, infrastructure and the transportation system. To know what type of services and programmes are available can be very useful to small start-up firms in the local community;

o Based on an analysis of the information the team has to design the future business incubator. It has to finally determine the purpose and the tasks of the incubator, the type of tenant it will house, and the type and location of the incubator. The team has also to make a business plan for the incubator;

o The team will need to define the resources available to start the incubator and must also find a site. The incubator building has to be large enough to produce rent revenue to generate cash flow, and break even or cover losses by other revenues. Donation funds and sponsors may also need to be identified, too;

o Considerable care should be taken in selecting the management. The manager or director has a key role in the success of the incubator. The success or failure of an incubator may depend on the qualities and performance of its director and also the amount of time he or she is able to spend with client businesses. An incubator director should be chosen especially for his or her ability to work with entrepreneurs and to help them grow their companies. The director should in particular be fully familiar with entrepreneurship and business development. Usually a business incubator also needs a secretary, a part-time custodian, bookkeepers, lawyers, an insurance agent, and a banker;

o Creating a business incubator takes from one to two years. Once the business incubator is operating, the revenue from the tenants should cover the running costs. Some services and training can be offered to entrepreneurs outside the incubator, thereby generating additional revenue. Any surplus earned should be reinvested in the centre;

o The criteria of sustainability can be divided into two categories: the management of the premises (real estate) and the support to tenants and reaching of maturity;

o The management of the premises is a commercial matter and an undertaking in itself. An incubator has to be operated in such a way that the common expenses are recovered through rent and other service charges. Since most business incubators are established for the development of local areas, it is crucial to gain financial, moral and public support from local municipalities and communities;

o The estimation of capital and operating costs should be based on a realistic assumption of expenses and revenue to enable the business incubator to break even after the initial start-up period. From a financial point of view, practice shows that it takes from three to five years for a business incubator to become self-sustainable. It appears that best practice in business incubators occurs when start-up enterprises and existing companies are mixed. This encourages mutual learning and provides a stimulating environment for beginning enterprises;

o The effectiveness of business incubators should be evaluated based on the number of successful companies that reach maturity and continue doing business outside the nurturing premises. The success of emerging companies creates a positive view of entrepreneurship and contributes to the creation of a new enterprise culture. Thereby, business incubators aspire to have a positive impact on their community's economic health.

Additional principles in some UN/ECE member countries include the following:

Azerbaijan

Azerbaijan feels that it needs to develop its own infrastructure policy in order to create a favourable environment. There is also a great need for more liberal legislation concerning taxation and investments policies.

Czech Republic

A Business Incubator is a tool for practical help and assistance to emerging entrepreneurs and business and a support system with financing from the national Phare programmes and the State Budget, offering a complete range of logistic services, including providing the office space and technology equipped facilities for manufacturing SMEs.

The activities of a business incubator are aimed at creating an entrepreneurial environment for companies. The firms in an incubator are provided with the services they need. They can be supported with contributions from a government programme or, for example, from resources of the Phare programme. As a result, a large number of small enterprises with serious interest can be placed in incubators. The choice of firms is made according to exact rules, the most important of which being the level of innovation, the quality of the business plan, the quality of the product and the way the production is based on research and development. The length of their presence in an incubator is important too - usually it is 3 years and exceptionally up to 5 years, with the last 2 years without financial support.

Finland

Establishing a business incubator is no simple task. It can be divided into at least the following stages:

o undertaking a feasibility study;
o drawing up a business plan for the incubator with a programme to launch the operations and finance the incubator until it becomes self-supporting;
o selecting a manager and a board of directors able to develop the incubator as a business and to help enterprises in incubation;
o finding suitable premises, which make it possible to run profitable business;
o establishing such shared services as are profitable for the tenant enterprises;
o building up a network, of producers of other services, financiers, educational establishments and enterprises.

Georgia

Georgia needs to develop its own strategic, economic and taxation models to support innovative business and the development of entrepreneurship in the country. Entrepreneurship must be protected from heavy taxation and excessive regulation. However, it is not in the power of an incubator, a technopark, or their managers to establish such protection, but rather the Government's role to take the necessary measures. As an example, the Centre for Enterprise Restructuring and Management Assistance has made a proposal to the Government on a tax-free zone with a tax moratorium for the Business Park for the first three to five years for an appropriate consultant to the Electoaparati plant.

Germany

The guiding principles are direct consequences of the definitions given above. On this basis innovation centres:

o are aimed at promoting start-up and development of enterprises (not promoting technology development);
o focus on start-up businesses with an entrepreneurial concept, a business plan (including all necessary components) and provide support to develop such business plans;

o are not for profit (because of the aim to support regional economic development).

Hungary

The most important principles are:

o an incubation period of a start-up enterprise for a maximum of five years:
o priority to start-up enterprises that meet the criteria as set forth for dynamic development, including employment, and innovation.

The first phase is to meet the criteria of an industrial park. This ensures that local development projects fit into the regional development plans as stipulated by the authorities, owners and the territory, as appropriate. The qualified candidates are authorized to apply for financial support and preferential treatment as set forth in the rules of the park.

The second phase is the application to obtain investment support for the infrastructure. Non-repayable state subsidies of 25 - 75 % are available for construction works. If an industrial park is established in a rural region, the maximum rate of the State subsidy is 75%.

Interest-free loans are available for investment inside the industrial park. Local Governments can provide further support to establish and run an industrial park, e.g. through local tax exemption.

Applications are reviewed centrally in a process involving the representatives of ministries, chambers of commerce and industry, lobby groups representing organizations and financial institutions. In the beginning, the progress of the industrial park programme was very slow as the concept was new in the country. A number of administrative constraints were removed and today there are 75 industrial parks with a total territory of 4,400 hectares operating in every region of the country.

There are 566 mostly small and medium-sized enterprises in the industrial parks. Based on the number of jobs created, the role of the industrial parks in job creation is advantageous and increasing. The total capital amounts to Ft 250 billion, equivalent to US$ 1 billion. It has created a turnover of Ft 700 billion, 70 % of which come from exports.

Italy

The choice of enterprise must be very rigid. They must be enterprises with strong growth potential. Generally speaking, they are enterprises with great interest in innovation, high tech and internationalization.

In the traditional sense, the enterprises oriented in this direction are the most vulnerable ones, since the results of their work come to light after a long time. This is the only reason why, generally speaking, public administrations are interested in supporting such activities which otherwise would be difficult to carry out by the entrepreneurs alone.

The most important problems a young entrepreneur has to cope with for the development of his/her own enterprise during the incubation phase are the following:
o the utilization of modular spaces which facilitate growth opportunities for the enterprise;
o access to services offered by consultancy firms at accessible costs;
o developing a network of commercial and technological partners;
o improving the managerial skills of the enterprise according to the production, market and services involved;
o identifying and activating the financial resources for the investments, advertising, distribution network, etc.

As regards the parameters for evaluating the success of an incubator two main characteristics need to be borne in mind:
o the benefits for the local community;
o the efficiency with which the resources for producing such benefits have been utilized.

The following check list is indicative and lists the parameters which should be used for realistic assessment over a period of time lasting not less than three years:
o new enterprises created;
o spin-offs from enterprises;
o enterprises attracted from outside the region;
o new jobs created;
o the mortality rate of the assisted firms ;
o enterprises expelled from the incubator;
o the total sum of investments generated in the assisted enterprises;
o the turnover of the assisted enterprises;
o the added value created by the enterprises;
o the profits of the assisted enterprises;

o the sales proceeds the enterprises make outside the region;

o the eventual creation of a risk capital fund.

The incubator has a social function and, in fact, enterprise promotion is not an end in itself but rather a solution to the unemployment problems which have an extremely high cost, both in terms of the contributions which Governments pay the unemployed and the consequent problems involved, such us free medical assistance, crime, social-welfare expenses and so on.

Latvia

First of all, an incubator needs to be able to provide complex services to its tenants. Every innovation support structure, including technological centres and parks, is an instrument for innovative activity. It must help small innovative enterprises to introduce new products, new production methods, new markets, new sources of inputs, and new forms of organization.

An incubator can only be operated on a non-profit basis. The invested capital is not to be repaid and no profit is to be generated. At the same time the necessary funds to cover operational costs have to be generated from the income.

The Advisory Board must exercise control over the use of the office and workshop space of the incubator.

Republic of Moldova

Owing to the very low level of entrepreneurial activity, all SMEs are allowed to enter a business incubator. Only insolvent enterprises, or those that do not conform with environmental, health and security requirements, are not allowed or are expelled.

The business incubator needs to meet its objectives and targets. Thus, to ensure a legal and regulatory framework for the incubators, the Government and other stakeholders need to develop special rules. For instance, a special expert commission of the incubator will select the applicants for the incubator according to the following criteria:

o availability of an initial product or service project;

o availability of at least a draft of a business plan;

o availability of an action plan for operating within the incubator;

o commitment of the applicant to the project and readiness to bear the minimum expenses.

At the start-up stage of the incubator, all the applicants are selected on condition that they must cover some minimum expenses (stationary, fax and similar). Once the applicants become tenants of the incubator, they can benefit from all the services provided, which will facilitate the development and implementation of the business idea. The SMEs can be incubated for a certain incubation period. After the business incubation period, the companies can operate independently.

Poland

Incubation services can be rendered to both growing companies and beginning ones. However, Business Support Centres, Industrial Zones and Special Economic Zones are not Business Incubaors in Poland. Thus, the general entrance criteria, such as those listed at the beginning of the chapter, are not applied for the last-mentioned organizations.

Russian Federation

We consider a business incubator first of all as a very effective tool for local economic activity revitalization. The flexibility of this economic model allows adjusting each incubator to serve regional needs and needs of small businesses the best possible way.

Therefore, we think that business incubators should:

o base their activity and services on local needs and conditions, and be market-oriented;

o work in cooperation with different regional players, gain support of local municipalities as a critical condition for success;

o base their work on intensive usage of previously unclaimed local resources;

o strive for self-sufficiency as the only condition for survival in the long term, and base their activity on business principles;

o carefully balance long-term financial tasks with the objectives of small-business support.

Slovakia

Special attention is given to innovative companies. The support is rendered in two phases.

In the selection process a business plan is developed for the company and the decision on accepting the company into an incubator is made. In the incubation process, a range of services that the company needs is made available. The average time of incubation is about three years.

Sweden

The incubator-system is available only for knowledge-intensive and research/technology-based spin-offs from universities or companies. When it comes to evaluating the business ideas we try to be very positive when offering places in the pre-incubator programme. That means that we seldom take a critical or evaluative stance during the time the start-ups are taking part in the entrepreneurship programme. But the programme is demanding. At this stage, we leave the evaluation to the market, the only relevant evaluator, as we see it. The pre-incubator programme is a matter of letting as many as possible test their ideas for a 12-month period.

The second stage, the regular incubator, is focused on helping start-ups with business in software or hardware development up to a maximised level of 5-6 people and a period of two-three years. The regular incubator is also open for entrepreneurs that do not take part in the entrepreneurship programme. Although we continue to encourage the companies, we also expose them to many more critics who take the time to evaluate the business plans and who help to further the development of the companies.

The ownership of the start-ups is important. Some incubators only offer space in the incubator activities for companies that are to 100% owned by the persons in the company. Some do not support start-ups partly owned by venture capitalists, universities, or larger firms. Naturally, these companies are offered space in the science park, but not in the incubator. We recognize that there are some important exceptions also. Smaller companies from abroad looking to establish a presence in Scandinavia or Northern Europe can sometimes access space in the incubators in order to start up here. These companies are provided a variety of resources related to the rather special situations that arise in internationalisation.

As one of the basic principles is to make the entrepreneurs think in a more business-oriented way; and to make them develop their entrepreneurial spirit, it is for them to take part in different activities

promoting business development. This is a part of the contract.

Turkey

An incubator must be an independent entity operating as a non-profit organization and established in accordance with the business plan approved by KOSGEB. The facilities and services to be provided for the tenants include independent work spaces, common facilities and counselling.

KOSGEB funds are available for the refurbishment of an incubator, including office equipment and operating expenses (with a decreasing rate of cost reimbursement for three to four years). A business plan must be prepared with a view to attaining self-sustainability.

KOSGEB evaluates the performance of the incubator according to a set of indicators including the financial state of the incubator, number of new ventures and jobs created, and the performance of the client companies.

Ukraine

The business incubator is expected to have the following features:
- o it is customized for Ukraine to provide delivery of incubator-like services to the hinterlands;
- o it is created by the BID programme based on proven techniques;
- o it uses the incubator paradigm as best one can over the web;
- o existing or prospective entrepreneurs apply for services (register) to be accepted as clients;
- o business education is provided as distance learning with a business-plan theme;
- o human consulting would be provided via e-mail or phone;
- o efforts are made to provide access to capital: information on loans, venture capital, etc.;
- o a website is created for each as the cyber equivalent of physical space; such as renting of physical space, this web-hosting model provides a revenue stream that can sustain the incubator;
- o e-commerce help is offered for posting of catalogues, shopping cart, credit cards, etc.
- o clerical services such as answering the

phone, access to a fax, i.e. forwarding of messages, change of media (convert email to fax, mail, etc.) packing of physical shipments, customs broker services;

o when a critical mass of clients is achieved in a town, a branch physical incubator can be created there to carry the economic development further.

CHAPTER 3

OBJECTIVES OF BUSINESS INCUBATION

Business incubators are growing rapidly over the world, from 200 at the beginning of the 1990s to over 3,000 today all over the world. The number of business parks in countries in transition is also growing every year. There are currently 60 business incubators in Russia. In the Czech Republic the number of business incubators amounts to more than 20, to 35 in Hungary, and to almost 60 in Poland.

The majority of the countries in transition (CITs) have acknowledged that private entrepreneurship is crucial for economic growth, and an important element of the reform process. Governments in the CITs also play a crucial role in the development of support services for enterprises. Some of these support institutions are in a beginning phase, while some institutions have acquired a vast experience of both success and failure. Many of these support institutions are newcomers to the market economy, lack entrepreneurial skills and need human and financial resources to be effective. One of the aims of this publication is to make some of these experiences in a number of UN/ECE member countries available for exchange between similar organizations to draw lessons for the future.

Among the various support institutions, business incubators, innovation centres, industrial parks and technoparks have proved to be effective instruments for assisting entrepreneurs in starting a business, nurturing young enterprises, and helping them to survive during the start-up period when they are most vulnerable.

In the last decade business incubators have been attracting increasing attention from indigenous policy makers, academicians, economists, and also donors and international organizations. The reason for this is that both in developed and developing countries as well as in countries in transition, small and medium-sized enterprises constitute a significant economic actor and contribute significantly to gross domestic product and new job creation. From a political and social point of view, Governments and international donors consider assistance to small and medium-sized enterprises as an instrument for economic growth and poverty alleviation through self-employment. It is also seen as a means of strengthening the private sector and a way to foster the reduction of regional disparities through decentralized local or regional development.

In the majority of the countries in transition, there is a lack of support services to enterprises. Even though Governments have already set for themselves the goal of developing entrepreneurship, support to the private sector, and the promotion of the infrastructure is rather weak and still at an infant stage.

The experiences of some advanced market economies, such as the European Union members and the United States of America, demonstrate that special emphasis should be put on beginner or start-up enterprises. In many cases a self-educated start-up entrepreneur is fully occupied with the development of the primary business, while she/he is badly in need of support services to implement the idea.

Are business incubators, industrial and technoparks an effective tool for SME development? What are the conditions that need to be in place for these initiatives to survive and flourish? How are business incubators sustainable and upon what do they depend? The Expert Meeting raised these questions, and these best practice guidelines will try to explain how different countries have answered some of them.

SPICE Group

The aims of innovation centres depend on the goals of the initiators and the stakeholders. The most general and typical goals include:

- creation of wealth;
- creation of jobs;
- diversification of the regional economic structure;
- promotion of (technology based) start-upenterprises;
- diffusion and application of new technologies;
- increased profit.

Azerbaijan

The first and primary objective is the development of small and medium-sized enterprises sector in Azerbaijan.

Bulgaria

In the Bulgarian National Strategy on the development of high technologies high technology parks (HTPs) form a focus of two important interrelated preconditions for sustainable economic development: tools of the Government for implementing policies on the development of the high technology sector, and on the other hand, tools for implementing policies regarding a competitive, innovative SME sector oriented towards a market based on high-tech products.

Depending on its organizational structure, management, specialization, size and the needs of the region or city concerned, the concept of a HTP is entirely or partially identical with the concepts of a Scientific Centre, Technical Centre, Technical Corridor or Technopole. The HTPs are expected to provide opportunities for a direct transfer of new research products from universities and R&D units to the markets. It is extremely important that they should help attract capital for the development of new market-oriented areas, given the specific "concentrated" intellectual capacity, encouraging innovation and entrepreneurship and providing greater possibilities for attracting risk capital. They should develop and maintain high quality information and telecommunications services, shared use of available infrastructure, technological resources, etc.

According to the National Strategy and the draft law on high technology activities and high technology parks, high technology parks encompassing technological incubators as a very important element, shall be established based on the structures and resources available in the country. They must have premises ensuring favourable conditions for the development, introduction and marketing of modern technologies and for research and development projects of scientific, research and educational establishments, technology companies, private entrepreneurs and investors, national and local Governments.

Croatia

The objectives of the business incubation and technology centres are:to

- support new technology based companies;
- create jobs for qualified employees;
- support commercialization of the innovations;

- o promote national technology, products and services;
- o attract FDI and joint ventures;
- o support the clustering processes;
- o support regional development;
- o strengthen national competitiveness;
- o enhance international networking.

The following preconditions should be meet in successful business incubation:

- o premises large enough to allow the incubator reach the financial break-even point;
- o incubation of clusters of firms in selected business area to reach the critical mass of firms with an impact on the local or regional economy incubation of the network of firms - i.e. a range of interconnected firms with complementary businesses and skills capable of offering complex services and solving problems that cannot be solved at the level of an individual firm;
- o various stimulating measures (financial, fiscal, administrative) for fostering entrepreneurship and export-oriented businesses;
- o a maximum of openness to foreign investment and international joint ventures;
- o capable management team skilled in technology assessment, business management, etc. with good connections with governmental and other institutions (e.g. banks, international organizations, etc.).

Czech Republic

The overall objective is to contribute to the improvement of economic development in the Czech Republic through the growth of small and medium-sized enterprises and to stabilize the SME sector, which produces more than 50 % of GDP and creates new jobs. The specific objective is to provide support to start-up entrepreneurs under favourable terms and to increase the quality of the activities.

The objectives of business incubation are formulated by the Society of Science and Technology Parks (SSTP, http://www.svtp.cz/svtpmain.htm), one of the founding organizations of the Association of Innovative Entrepreneurship of the Czech Republic (AIE CR, http://www.aiecr.cz). Established in 1990, the SSTP is a union of legal entities and individuals that support efficient innovation processes. Currently, there are 20 science and technology parks or BICs

accredited by the SSTP and further applications are being processes.

The detailed objectives of individual science and technology parks or BICs differ according to their origin, human resources, material and technical equipment available, the stage of the development and also the regional needs and opportunities. A majority of the parks have emerged during the transformation process of former research and development institutes. Sometimes, they are a product of private initiatives of individuals or groups such as research departments or project teams that spin-off from larger organizations, e.g. State-owned enterprises or research institutes.

The newly formed institutions operate as independent non-profit or commercial organizations. Sometimes, the former parent institutions support the new ones by providing them with cheaper or free premises, including offices, production space, laboratories, instruments and equipment.

Finland

The basic idea is to develop a more favourable local business environment for targeted types of new enterprise. Business incubation is a programme that provides entrepreneurs with appropriate premises, equipment, shared services and advice, contacts and specialist services. But the concept varies considerably according to local circumstances.

In Finland, a wide-ranging survey of business incubation has been carried out recently. The survey gives a good picture of the views of the managers on the operation of the business incubators. According to the survey the most important objective of business incubation is to create jobs. Another important objective is to contribute to the diversification of the business structure. There are further complementary objectives relating to international trade, regional economy, particular objective sectors and entrepreneurship.

Among operational objectives, linking small enterprises to bigger firms and establishing cooperation among enterprises in general are emphasized. A further objective is to help entrepreneurs develop their skills. Speeding up the growth of enterprises and strengthening the local economy are closely related to this. Other objectives include increasing access to finance, providing entrepreneurial training, facilitating the creation of spin-offs and providing favourable conditions for start-ups.

As for the character of the operations of business incubators, one third have tenants operating in several fields of business, and one third are specialized in technology firms (high-tech firms account for more than a half of the tenants). Service-intensive incubators account for 13 per cent. Finnish business incubators are clearly more focused on technology than those in the United States, where the share of technology-oriented businesses is one fourth. Business incubators are often considered creators of "spearhead firms" in new high-tech sectors. About 50 per cent of business incubators are linked to a university or polytechnic. However, they also represent the commercial sector, as well as art and design. Another big group of business incubators operates closely with a local or regional development centre. New forms of incubation include, for instance, business incubators in the fields of tourism and rural businesses.

Almost every other incubator has a municipality or an organization of municipalities as its principal owner. Other typical owners are educational establishments and technology centres or joint projects of the institutions mentioned. Private limited liability companies account for 9 per cent of incubator owners. Therefore, incubation business is to a great extent an instrument of the regional industrial policy, and on the other hand a way for educational establishments and other institutions to create a channel enabling the transformation of their expertise into new business operations.

According to the experience gained in Finland, business incubators established in a university environment may offer the students, teachers and others the best chance for the creation of enterprises, especially when it is a part of an extended science park or a centre of expertise. Preconditions for successful operations are suitable premises, sufficient supply of high quality services, and especially a strong network of contacts to secure the choice of suitable ideas and entrepreneurs for incubation and the supply of financial and other support services.

A business incubator may also be a good practice measure in the development of business environment in other local business centres. In such a case, the number of enterprises involved is smaller, but the support services provided by the incubator and the favourable conditions for the establishment of cooperation between enterprises offer better

opportunities to start new types of business. But to be successful, an incubator needs a clear strategy and a profile. A precondition for this is a sufficient supply of business ideas and potential entrepreneurs in the region concerned.

To summarize, the critical points for success of an incubator are:

- o start supported by strong local partners, based on a feasibility study and a business plan;
- o independent corporation, but part of a larger local structure for development;
- o well managed business with clear objectives, being self-sustaining after an initial period;
- o location and premises suitable for the chosen strategy and for profitable operation;
- o diverse supply of business services at a reasonable cost by establishing own shared services and a network for other services;
- o strategy-based selection of new tenants and work for graduation phase provides success for incubator and for the new enterprises.

Georgia

The development of small and medium-sized enterprise sector in Georgia is one of the priorities of the Government's economic policy.

The main task today is to develop support mechanisms for small and medium-sized enterprises and enhance competition and free entrepreneurship in the country. Business incubation, as one tool, can provide entrepreneurs with appropriate premises, equipment and shared services.

The first step was taken in Georgia in May-June 1999, when Georgia's first business park (incubator) was established. The business park was founded by the Centre for Enterprise Restructuring and Management Assistance (CERMA), a project financed by the World Bank. The goal was to create facilities matching western standards utilizing the premises of "Electro-aparati", an existing plant.

Germany

Business incubators in general can be set up for very different objectives. Therefore a clear definition of goals and tasks is an important part of any business plan for an incubator. Based on the defined set of aims, the objectives can be described.

Typical general aims include the following:
o   creation of wealth;
o   diversification of the regional economic structure;
o   promotion of (technology) start-up enterprises;
o   diffusion/application of new technologies;
o   creation of jobs;
o   profit.

In other words, the aim is to contribute to the revitalization of an abandoned industrial (or military) site, help unemployed people to discover entrepreneurship as an alternative or to promote the transfer of technology (from a research institution) by transferring people to new companies. The concrete tasks and working patterns are determined by the interests of the institution initiating and/or operating the incubator. A university, for example, will put emphasis on technology-based activities, on transfer of technology, a local regional development agency will stress the entrepreneurial approach in general (any kind of company is good for job creation) and a financial or venture capital institution will focus on profits. All such kinds of incubator exist in Germany - usually in a mixed form, that is with a combination of institutions as shareholders and consequently with a mixture of expectations and aims.

Hungary

The incubator programme was initiated by the SEED Foundation in 1990. It was assisted financially by the PHARE SME programme and the Hungarian Foundation for Enterprise Promotion in 1991.

The objectives of the Hungarian incubator house programme are to provide small and medium-sized enterprises with basic services and premises at a reasonable cost and to provide other services using various instruments of enterprise development such as consultancy, training and micro-credit. These concentrated services have allowed an entrepreneurial spirit to develop fast. During the first few years, the incubators were creations of the Local Enterprise Centres backed up by the PHARE SME programme.

The Industrial Park Programme is based on three pillars:
o   The objective of business incubators is to support new enterprises, which are vulnerable due to exposure to strong competition;
o   Business incubators are one of the strongest instruments in regional development;
o   Innovation and science parks constitute the basis for research and development.

In Hungary, the conditions for launching an industrial park programme were created in mid 1996. The local Governments realized that the start-up and survival of SMEs in their region should be supported in a concerted manner in respect of employment, investment promotion and enterprise development.

Most local Governments possess territories requiring development of their real estate features owing to the termination of their former activity. One of the most suitable uses of these industrial establishments was to establish an industrial park. The industrial programme was thus started in 1996 to link local, regional and economic and political goals.

Italy

The incubator has one short-term objective, and one medium and long-term objective. The short-term objective is to create enterprises by means of supplying the basic and advanced services mentioned beforehand, in order to be a natural reference point for those young entrepreneurs needing helpful information such as:
o   creating and making visible a critical number of small enterprises. This critical mass of small enterprises helps those in charge of the incubator to relate to the Public Administration and so create conditions useful for the development of small enterprises, such as the creation of guarantee funds, seed capital funds, facilitated bank loans, and tax relief;
o   preparing the enterprises for their start-up outside the incubator;
o   acting as the link between the world of research and innovation and the world of enterprises.

The medium and long-term objective however, should be:
o   the creation of innovative enterprises;
o   promotion on a large scale for high-tech enterprises and spin-offs of enterprises from the firms.

Kyrgyzstan

The goals of business incubation in Kyrgyzstan are:
o the development of small and medium-sized enterprises;
o a decrease in unemployment through job generation;
o improved well-being for people through a higher standard of living.

Latvia

The goals of the newly created structures are to promote cooperation among scientific research institutions, industrial and trade enterprises; to help meet the demands of the market led economy; and to help establish small technologically oriented private enterprises. Besides, these structures can offer small and medium-sized enterprises not only infrastructure services but also consultation on business planning, marketing, quality management, market research, international cooperation, etc. Thus, experts on science parks and innovation centres are trying to help SMEs to overcome problems such as:
o insufficient assets;
o domestic market is too narrow for SMEs, especially for high-tech companies;
o lack of start-up and investment capital;
o property and ownership problems;
o lack of information;
o insufficient experience, knowledge and entrepreneurial skills.

Republic of Moldova

The objectives of business incubation are:
o orient start-up enterprises in line with the priority branches of the respective region's economy
  - manufacture of high-quality products high-competitiveness on internal and external markets
  - elaboration and implementation of new technologies
  - development of market infrastructure;
o access to facilities for founders of enterprises that suit the needs of newly created enterprises;
o provision to start-up enterprises of services including auxiliary facilities, consulting and training;

o support to enterprises in the search for new markets, partners and funds.

Poland

There are several fields in which business incubation centres (BICs) can play an important role in the local economy:

o Job creation. People who have lost their jobs can establish firms and develop private businesses for self-employment. Operational firms can also enter a BIC to develop new activities to increase the number of their employees;
o Increasing investment opportunities. New businesses explore undiscovered market segments, which can be profitably invested in and the first opportunity for local investors is often an investment in a BIC. Often the centre is located in a new building. In addition, the facility, regardless of size and age, is a visiting card of a construction firm and the architect;
o Diversifying the economy. New entrepreneurs compete with existing firMs They tend to find products and services that are not yet in the market, which, in turn, may diversify the local economy;
o Tax generation. Well-functioning firms and their subcontractors generate tax revenue;
o Improved competitiveness. New and developing firms can find niches and new market segments, thus filling a gap between the supply by local businesses and the demand of local, national and international clients;
o Alternative employment opportunities. Spin-off companies and unemployed people starting their own business usually have to learn new skills particularly as regards business management. Furthermore, firms creating new products and services very often generate demand for new professionals;
o Complementing programmes for local development. Privatization and restructuring of the local economy as well as other specialized programmes are complemented by BICs, which can organize training, create network of manufacturers, use idle buildings, prepare employment projects for laid-off workers, etc.

Russian Federation

Worldwide experience proves that business incubators are able not only to assist small business growth but also to have complex impact on local community development. Business incubator serves as intersystem communicator between small business and other economic forces of a region. As a rule, a business incubator involves labour, production, technological, financial and other regional resources, working in coordination with big corporations, local administrations and educational institutions.

A business incubator as an economic development model can serve the revival of economic activity in general and/or can influence certain components of it. Business incubators can easily be inserted into different regional infrastructure and can carry out different sets of economic development functions, depending on local conditions and needs. They can serve interests of different social groups and organizations, such as society as the whole, small business communities, governmental structures and local authorities, industrial corporations, educational institutions etc.

Among business incubator objectives the following major groups can be pointed out:
- o Economic development (regional development, industrial diversification, job creation, taxation base expansion etc.)
- o The following subcategories marked out in this group:
  - Community development
  - Enterprises development (mostly aimed at job creation)
  - Development of certain market sectors or groups of clients (work in a certain sector, such as food processing - kitchen incubators, clothing - apparel incubators, crafts, microbiology etc. or with specific groups as ethnic minorities, young people, women etc.)
- o Technology commercialization (usually university based)
- o Commercial objectives (real estate development or venture enterprises)
- o Combination of previously mentioned approaches (usually there more that one objective such as enterprise development and commercial interests.

Slovakia

In order to provide professional support services to small and medium-sized entrepreneurs the National Agency for Development of Small and Medium Enterprises created a network that includes Regional Advisory and Information Centres (RAIC) and Business and Innovation Centres (BIC).

The Government of Slovakia initiated the network in cooperation with the European Union within the framework of the Phare Small and Medium Enterprises Programme for the Czech and Slovak Federal Republic signed in October 1991. The centres were created in selected areas according to the following criteria:
- o priority region with ongoing industrial restructuring that has led to a decrease in employment;
- o large centres offering sufficient potential for the development of modern innovative enterprises.

The BICs were the first instrument for supporting small and medium-sized enterprises in Slovakia. The conditions for traditional founders of BICs in the European Union, such as cities, regions, chambers of commerce and entrepreneurs, did not exist in Slovakia and, therefore, a private limited liability company (s.r.o.) was established in Bratislava as a spin-off of a research institute. Between 1993 and 1996 the network expanded to 12 RAICs and 5 BICs, the latter of which include business incubators.

The BICs are non-profit-making organizations established as limited liability companies, in which the profit is not distributed. In case any profit is made, it is utilized for company development and the support of entrepreneurs. The flexibility of a limited liability company allows to develop activities and secure financing for them through grants as well as with the financial results of the company's own entrepreneurial activities.

The main task of the BIC is searching and selecting of small and medium-sized enterprises, eventually starting entrepreneurs, whose business plans are innovative (launching a new product, service or technology). They create favourable conditions for those innovative companies by providing them with a special long-term care (2-3 years) and serve as "incubators" helping to reduce the inevitable start-up costs.

This work should contribute to the restructuring, recovery and economic development of the region by mobilising the regional potential in technical, scientific, financial, logistical and human resources areas. The BIC's work includes the search, evaluation, selection and orientation of innovation projects of entrepreneurs able to found and conduct their own business, with high potential of added value. The BICs also support enterprises with projects to implement a new entrepreneurial body or a production process in an existing enterprise.

Sweden

Incubation activity in Sweden concentrates on helping spin-offs and new start-ups from universities and other higher education and research establishments that are generating projects with a high potential for commercialisation. Often, the entrepreneurial spirit embodied in those who initiate these opportunities for Commercialisation is not enough to help them develop the business and run a company. Sweden's incubators are designed to provide these new entrepreneurs with the support and expertise they need in order to launch their businesses successfully.

Very often an incubator is a part of a Science or Technology Park, the optimal environment for companies with large growth potential. But today, one can also find a growing number of student-based start-up initiatives. Often, these are found in cities with younger universities and no Science or Technology Park, and also in larger cities with no park-related incubator.

Another type of incubator is an in-house incubator in a company, where a single (larger) company forms an incubator for stimulating new ideas and projects. This serves to stimulate the entrepreneurial spirit among the employees and a higher level of innovation as well. Although some projects may remain with the larger company, most will spinout from the company particularly if the project has a focus outside of the company's core business.

The main objective of incubators is to make it easier for start-ups to maximise their growth potential. The premises are nothing more than just a tool among other tools. The goal for incubators is to develop companies, not real estates. In Sweden we talk about environments – total environments that support knowledge–intensive business ideas to become growing companies. These environments provide access to different services as well as advice and mentors. The environment also stimulates networking between the companies in the incubator

as well as with more mature companies outside. Ultimately, the new companies benefit from their successful development and the whole community – universities, businesses, residents – benefit from the generation of broader clusters of technical expertise, new jobs and greater wealth.

Ukraine

To design the project on Best United States Practices that Can be Adapted to Ukraine, a formal review of best practices in the United States was made, and an intensive short course was organized in the United States in June 1998 to transfer those techniques to American and Ukrainian staff. In examining a number of incubators in the United States, a number of best practices emerge. While the following best practices cited is not an exhaustive list, they are the ones that seemed to have direct applicability to Ukraine.

o   Identify a champion. Successful incubator operations seem to be derived from a vision of groups of forward thinking business people who have a commitment to supporting small business in their community. Often the champion and implementers of the vision rests with economic development officers of states, counties, or cities. Financial and managerial support from the economic development offices provides the initial investment for physical facilities and then the managing director, who is the visible champion, creates the environment to attract small businesses to the incubator and sets the tone for its successful operation;

o   Establish a network of partners. Developing a network of alliances and partnerships with successful small businesses, government agencies, foundations, and educational institutions provides a wealth of varied skills and abilities to support the needs of the incubator and its clients. From these partners and sponsors, advisory boards may be created to provide on-going guidance and counselling to the managing director and to the incubator clients. Further, their financial support will assist in the sustainability of the incubator;

o   Determine a focus. For incubators to be most successful, an economic sector focus should be adopted based on a thorough and objective analysis of the needs of its community. In the United States common choices include: high technology, bio-technical, services, light manufacturing, agricultural products, consumer products, to name a few. This sector specialization helps to meet the local demand for assistance by entrepreneurs and small businesses, know the extent of financing and other resources, understand the markets available, and be sure of the availability of technical advice and access to it;

o   Provide Physical Space and Business Services. A physical structure for the incubator establishes an environment conducive to developing entrepreneurs and their enterprises. The incubator needs to establish an image and "look," "feel," and "taste" of a business location and offer quality, affordable space to attract start-ups and businesses with growth potential. Within the incubator a full list of business services is needed that are provided at low cost through sharing. While in some cases, an incubator without walls can be appropriate, a physical location for provision of quality, low cost business services is necessary;

o   Include formalized business education, training, and business plan development. Providing formalized business training is not standard among the incubators reviewed. In many instances, it is informal relying on individual entrepreneurs to seek assistance from the incubator or on the managing director detecting a need and suggesting the appropriate resources to the client firm. Still, the opportunity for success is enhanced where relationships with educational institutions or appropriate professional organizations, such as Service Corps of Retired Executives (SCORE), exist and regularly scheduled courses are offered. Integration of business plan development into training courses also seems to make a positive contribution;

o   Provide on-going business counselling. One of the most valuable components of being a tenant in an incubator or associated with an incubator, is the availability of on-going, in-depth business counselling. The opportunity for immediate feedback and

assistance leaves the firm with more time for productive work and reduces the number of costly erroneous decisions;

o   Provide access to capital. Incubators need to attract sufficient financial resources to ensure their sustainability. This can be a three to five year process. For sustainability of incubators, there are several models that have been implemented: (i) an up-front grant that covers the capital investment and operational expenses of the incubator for the start-up period; (ii) an up-front grant that covers the capital investment with operating expenses being covered through delivery of services; and (iii) sponsors make investments of 10 to 15 years in return for equity positions in the businesses with high growth potential and are willing to cover the expenses of the incubator until the positions are cashed. Incubator managing directors also need to attract financing for their clients. They do this through developing relationships with banking institutions, venture capitalists, foundations, and micro-enterprise loan institutions;

o   Camaraderie. Incubator clients share insights and their experiences in dealing with business problems. These relationships provide new entrepreneurs the opportunity of benefiting from the experienced business owners. It is helpful to provide a forum for a mix of clients, such as: (i) start-ups that show signs of success, (ii) successful fast-growing firms near graduation from the incubator, (iii) established businesses that may provide business services to other clients in the incubator and have no intention of graduating, and (iv) businesses that are candidates for the incubator, but are developing and the outlook for them is uncertain. Indeed one of the most useful services an incubator can provide is though its selection process, which can counsel prospective entrepreneurs that they should not proceed until they have a better business concept.

Uzbekistan

The development of small and private entrepreneurship is of great importance in the State economic policy of the Government of Uzbekistan.

In fact, the necessity to develop flexible small industrial structures and institutions of a service sphere capable of adequately responding to the market changes, has become the most important aspect of success because of the ever-increasing competition in the constantly changing world of today. In Uzbekistan, this is even more so as the Republic moves forward from a centrally planned economy to a dynamic market economy consisting of smaller flexible enterprises, which are now regarded as a key component in generating individual prosperity and employment.

However, the SME sector in Uzbekistan has a number of problems that hamper its development. These include insufficient capabilities of entrepreneurs to operate in market conditions, lack of knowledge of the principles of market economy (management, marketing, etc.) and legislation, lack of professional skills (computer literacy, book keeping, accounting, taxation, etc.), lack of information on prospective technologies and know-how and the absence of an entrepreneurial "culture". These kinds of problem are typical of newly established firms, managers of which only yesterday were engaged in occupations far removed from entrepreneurship.

A number of initiatives aimed at promoting small and medium-sized private entrepreneurship have therefore been created and stimulated by the Government. A system for SME support has been created, including a network of SME support institutions, tax reforms, an improvement of the banking system, promotion of foreign investments, appropriate normative and legal basis. A number of provisions for capital and venture funds providing access for entrepreneurs to credits in foreign currencies in an amount of more than $350 million has been included in the legislation. In addition, there is a variety of programmes on economic restructuring, including some implemented with the assistance of the United Nations.

The Government also strongly encourages the UNDP initiative to establish and promote business incubators as a means of nurturing entrepreneurial activity and to create more favourable environment to support small businesses.

As a result of the business incubator development programme of the UNDP, which was started in August 1994, three pilot incubators - two in Tashkent and one in Samarkand were established. Based on the experience gained, the Government took a decision (a resolution of the Cabinet of Ministers of the Republic of Uzbekistan 28 August 1995) to expand the programme in other regions of the country in order to stimulate entrepreneurial activity and economic growth.

Through the cooperation of the Committee for State Property and the UNDP, a network of 23 business incubators is already operational. The network of business incubators has brought about 3,000 jobs since 1996 and products and services have been produced for more than a billion sums (equivalent to US $ 110,000). Furthermore, four joint ventures have been set up with a total of fixed funds amounting to more than US $ 1 million. Assistance has been rendered to obtain preferential credits from Business Fund and other local financial institutions for more than sum 250 million. More than 7,000 people have been trained in market economy principles and professional skills.

The project has a clear objective - to support and develop small and medium-sized entrepreneurship in the country. The priority of the project is the creation of a favourable framework for the successful development of the tenants of the business incubators, including innovation, introduction of prospective up-to-date technologies into small businesses, the start-up and expansion of production and services to the tenants.

CHAPTER 4

BUSINESS ENVIRONMENT

The business environment of an incubator consists of two crucial factors: the immediate environment near the incubator and a more general business environment in the region and the country. When selecting a site for an incubator, there are a number of success factors that need to be taken into account. For instance, many local business assistance centres – business support centres, incubators, technoparks etc. – focus on a particular economic sector, often naturally based on the resources and skills available in the region concerned. However, each institution needs to take a stand as to the importance of the focus and differentiation: will they reject and attractive client, just because they are not strictly speaking within the chosen sector?

At the same time the financing bodies, the local and regional authorities, as well as the business communities, may have different priorities, particularly as regards the size of companies to be incubated, or, for instance, the services that need to be rendered.

The role and importance of the business environment of an incubator is seen in very different ways in different parts of Europe:

Azerbaijan

The main target of Azerbaijan is its integration to European structures. Thus, creating a favourable business environment is vital. One of the principal goals of Azerbaijan today is to shift investors' attention towards the non-oil sector of the economy, develop franchising and cooperation of SMEs with transnational corporations, as well.

The first step was taken recently, when the Academy of Sciences of Azerbaijan agreed to host an incubator. In addition, Bakmil, a big Azeri electronics factory, has also been interested in this project.

Bulgaria

A High Technology Park is expected to be a territory where the private sector meets with the public sector, the investor with potential beneficiaries, academic research institutes with applied research and products with markets. This is because the founders of a technology park can be:

o the Government with an initial contribution of shares owned directly by the Government or by governmental institutes, laboratories and similar facilities. The Government's contribution may also include land, real estate, direct financing and other assets
o municipalities with an initial contribution of land, buildings, facilities, and operating capital;
o higher educational establishments and the Academy of Sciences with an initial contribution of land, buildings, infrastructure systems, machines, equipment, money etc.;
o legal entities involved in high technology activities developing export-oriented hi-tech products and services. The contribution can be property as well as non-property rights and financing.

Being one of the priorities of the Government, the development and encouragement of the high technology activities and high technology parks is a responsibility of the Council of Ministers. The Government adopts a Development Strategy for the sector and the supporting Annual Programmes for its implementation.

To handle policies in high technologies under the guidance of the Minister of Economy, an Advisory Council is envisaged. Its members will be experts from other government agencies related to high technology development, as well as experts from both business and non-profit, non-governmental sectors. The Ministry of Economy will also set up a special unit, pursuing the high technology policies as set forth in the related legislation. One of its functions will be to keep a public register of high technology parks and their members.

An important part of the development of high technologies is the international support for Bulgaria's efforts in the sector through:

o international programmes (UNDP, OECD, etc.) and programmes of the international financial institutions (the World Bank, EBRD);
o the Fifth Framework Programme of the European Community for Research,

Technology and Demonstration; integration into which is extremely important for the preparation for full membership in the EU is given particular attention;

o long-term multilateral agreements (the Black Sea Economic Cooperation), bilateral technical assistance agreements (the US Agency for International Development, British Know How Fund, Japan, France, Netherlands and others);

o programmes of international private and public foundations;

o international high technology networks.

Croatia

Essential for the successful operation of business incubators and technology centres is the support of the local community and good relations with all supporting institutions such as universities, chambers of economy, local banks, ministries and so on. Business incubator and technology centres contribute to a better entrepreneurial climate in the surrounding area and give the impulse for everybody to start a business, to keep the business alive and to create new jobs, which is very important for the community.

Governmental supporting programmes are stimulating the creation of new and the development of existing SMEs. These supporting programmes for SMEs are primarily focused on:

o re-orientation of SMEs from trade towards productive and technology-based business;

o further development and strengthening of the SME sector within the national economy structure;

o encouraging private entrepreneurship and innovation culture in general.

The support programmes for SMEs in Croatia are under the responsibility of two State ministries: Ministry of Economy, whose support is aimed at all kinds of small privately owned firms and crafts, and the Ministry of Science and Technology for supporting technology-based business.

The Ministry of Economy started the programmes of promoting small entrepreneurship in 1996, which include the following activities:

o business assistance and expert consultations through the Croatian network of consultants, specially created for this purpose.

Government subventions for using the network services are also provided;

o initial financial resources for the small loans programme which is performed through the economy departments of local authorities - counties (the amount of initial resources is correlated with the amount of resources invested by local authorities);

o business management education of staff responsible for small business development at local authorities;

o nation-wide marketing campaign for the promotion and the encouragement of entrepreneurship.

The Ministry of Science and Technology (MOST) primarily supports technology-based firms i.e. firms based on new products, services or processes (which do not exist on the Croatian market and manufacturing). These firms could be classified as high-tech or technology advanced firms and usually belong to high technology sectors such as biotechnology, microelectronics, new materials, communication and information sciences. They could also originate from R&D activities at university/ research institutes or other kind of research institutions as their spin-offs. Therefore, MOST fosters the technology transfer and cooperation between the private sector of SMEs and the public research sector as well.

MOST is implementing two framework programmes for supporting technology-based SMEs:

o establishing of technology centres and similar institutions for the firm's incubation and technology transfer. Two technology centres and one centre for technology transfer have been established;

o ?creation and implementation of Government (administrative, legislative, fiscal, financial, etc.) stimulating measures for assisting SMEs. Within this programme the Business Innovation Centre of Croatia - BICRO was established to implement the mechanisms for financial support to SMEs at the national level, primarily through the financial institutions in a form of seed capital. In addition, the Government adopted the programme of Promoting and Starting Manufacturing Based on New Technologies in 1998. The Programme is aimed at equity investments in technology-based SMEs.

However, neither special financial institutions for innovative SMEs nor special financial funds for the development of new products or technologies exist yet in Croatia.

The other main characteristics of the business environment in Croatia are:

o   after the slow-down in the Croatian economy in 1999, a modest growth is forecasted for the year 2000;

o   an increase in FDI is expected, as well as a decrease in the costs of the capital;

o   low inflation and stable currency policy will be kept.

The purpose of the Small Business Zone is to enable local entrepreneurs to achieve cheaper working area, to keep the local working force close to their home, to raise the potential of the local community and to attract outside investors. The plan is to continue to develop small industrial zones in small municipalities around towns. Among others one reason is to avoid concentrating industry in any one place.

The starting point was to investigate and find an appropriate piece of land (maybe even in municipality ownership). The documentation of the project was then financed by the County. The County took the role of finding the best credit solution to build the zone. Future entrepreneurs are also participating in the whole cost, but without wasting their time with bureaucracy.

Four zones are planned. They will be situated in municipalities of Jelenje and Viškovo and the towns of Krk and Bakar. In the whole small business zone there will be one or few buildings. The buildings will be one-floor edifices divided in boxes and supplied with all the necessary infrastructure. The entrepreneurs can buy or rent one, two or more boxes according to need.

Czech Republic

The local and regional business environment plays a crucial role for science and technology parks and BICs. In addition, both the direct and indirect involvement of the Czech Government through its SME policy has also a very substantial role, particularly that of the Ministry of Industry and Trade (MIT), generally responsible for SME development.

The Ministry of Industry and Trade is generally responsible for SMEs promotion excluding regional enterprise promotion. The Ministry for Regional Development is responsible for SMEs

programme promotion of regional scope. The Czech-Moravian Guarantee and Development Bank was founded in 1992 for the implementation of promotion programmes developed by the above-mentioned ministries.

The Ministry of Agriculture provides assistance to the agroindustries, forestry and water economics through the Agricultural and Forestry Fund. The Ministry of Labour and Social Affairs provides indirect support to SMEs through different employment policy instruments, such as retraining support to job searchers etc.

Finland

In the Finnish SME policy, the present objective is to develop the business environment in the country. On a local level this means measures to promote such clusters of enterprises, as well as public and private services, which further enhance new entrepreneurship. Another objective of the Government's measures is the promotion of the competitiveness of small and medium-sized enterprises. Incubators are an important part in both these aspects.

Depending on the background of Finnish business incubators, two typical business environments exist: a) the business incubator as part of the concept of a centre of expertise, and b) the business incubator as part of other regional industrial policy. The business incubator often forms part of "a centre of expertise" comprising educational establishments and research institutions and possibly a science park. In the latter case, the benefits in the form of synergy and also status gained from operation within a central unit improve the preconditions for new entrepreneurial activities related to the centre's special fields of expertise. From the central unit's point of view, on the other hand, the business incubator provides the personnel with a new possibility, entrepreneurship, in an environment meeting a high standard. Owing to these benefits, business incubators have already become a regular part of the concept of a centre of expertise.

The results achieved by business incubators within science parks or technology centres linked up to technical universities have been very positive. Such a centre is able to provide both enterprises in incubation and other enterprises in the region with operating conditions and services of high quality. The whole formed by such a centre also makes it possible for service undertakings of different kinds, such as consultants, to operate within it. The association of Finnish science parks (FISPA) has 16 member centres. The number of persons working in science parks amounts to nearly 10,000. The association plays an important role in the development of business incubation.

The Finnish regional centres where there is a university are often examples of successful utilization of incubation as part of the local concept for promoting new knowledge-based enterprises. The following example of the structure of an incubator is based on the largest incubator in Finland and all the Nordic countries, located in Helsinki region.

Innopoli, a limited liability company owned by Finnish industries, the financing sector, research institutions and the city of Espoo is located near the Helsinki University of Technology and the Technical Research Centre of Finland. The company acts as a "generator" of new enterprises and owns a service centre and a main building containing service and business premises. A subsidiary, the Otaniemi Science Park, is responsible for the incubation and administration of the incubator premises. The operations are focused on high-tech information technology firms.

There is a separate programme, Spinno, which, in cooperation with universities in the Helsinki region and the government technology services for SMEs, aims at identifying ideas for new enterprises, and organising training for new firms and firms going international. Spinno-Seed Ltd carries on capital investment activities targeted at enterprises at seed and start-up stages in the Helsinki region and adjacent areas. Culminatum Ltd is a management company of the fund and also carries out the programme for centres of expertise in the region.

As regards business incubators established in other regional and local development centres, the importance of cooperation with existing companies needs to be emphasized: the incubator contributes to the creation of new services and subcontractors in the region and these incubators often profile themselves on the basis of an industrial sector. This form of activity is similar to that of industrial estates established as early as in the 1970s and, in particular, their reception facilities.

An example of these is the incubator at the Business Centre of south-western Häme. The incubator, with an area of 1,750 m2, has a dozen tenants and all the typical services and support networks. Located in a regional centre, it cooperates with the local technical college, as well as with different universities and science parks in south and central Finland. Its objective is to create jobs in the manufacturing industry and establish connections between the industry and the training organizations. Its tenants have so far created half of the jobs in the local electronic industry.

The importance of public and private services available in the adjacent area must, however, be emphasized. Access to and the quality of services available in the area are of vital importance to small firms and their successful operations.

As regards the results, business incubators are particularly effective in helping to establish firms and create jobs, as well as in developing cooperation between enterprises and educational establishments. Other important results include the commercialization of new technology and the improvement of the image of the community concerned. Even if the number of new businesses established in incubation is small as compared with all new enterprises, they have a very important role to play as spearheads of innovative businesses and as reformers of the local business structure and the supply of services.

Georgia

In order to enable the development of small businesses it is necessary to create a viable environment based on various components. The aim of Georgia is to become a transport corridor between east and west, connecting the Caucasian and the Central Asian countries with the Black Sea. The integration of the country in the European structures for scientific, technological and cultural cooperation is extremely important for the country's full integration in Europe.

Hungary

The SME policy of the Government is coordinated and partially financed by the Hungarian Foundation for Enterprise Promotion (HFEP) formed in 1990. The other half of the financial resources come from the Phare SME programme. The Network of Local Enterprise Agencies (LEA) was started in 1991 when the first experimental agencies were established in six counties.

The network of the Foundation was extended into six further counties between 1993 and 1994, and in 1995 there was already an agency in each county and the capital. The establishment and the operation of these agencies was promoted by the Foundation with resources from the Phare SME Programme and the Hungarian Government. One of the conditions was that each county was to establish the agency as a non-profit foundation, and then to annually draft business plans based on the structure and budget of the Term of Reference provided by the experts of the Foundation and the Phare programme.

In addition, there are initiatives, such as industrial parks that are only partially connected to the activities of the local enterprise agencies.

Italy

Over the years, both the national and the Regional Governments have created a tight network of institutions which support policies in favour of SMEs and each of these originally had a specific role. Taking into consideration the most important ones only, the institutions which support SMEs on a national level are as follows:

o The Ministry of Industry handles Law 488, which finances investments for the building of industrial sheds and the acquisition of machinery by allocating contributions of free loans of up to 65% of the entire investment;

o The Institute of Foreign Trade, which deals with supporting activities for those enterprises wishing to export to foreign countries or make investments abroad;

o La Compagnia Finanziaria Italiana (The Italian Finance Company), which intervenes in favour of companies in recession and also finances the setting-up of new companies formed by the employees of the company in recession (who would otherwise be unemployed), who then take over the management of the company's activities;

o ENISUD deals with the promotion and management of the companies in recession regarding productive reconversion programmes, plus industrial initiatives;

o ITAINVEST S.p.a. is a merchant bank whose social capital is entirely public and which finances the risk capital of private, Italian

and foreign companies which do not have enough funds to cover an investment and therefore invest in new entrepreneurial initiatives in Italy;

o Imprendidorialità Giovanile S.p.a. (Young Entrepreneurship S.p.a.), which deals with the creation of new enterprises, set up by young entrepreneurs by financing the building of industrial sheds plus the acquisition of machinery. This institution grants free loans of up to 65% and easy-term financing of up to 25%. These are granted on condition that the entrepreneurs participate in a two-month training course. The course precedes the granting of the investment, and, moreover, the companies involved also benefit from financing which covers the running costs during the first three years of activity with decreasing percentages;

o INSUD deals with the promotion and development of tourist enterprises by participating in risk capital of companies which operate in the hotel trade sector and services and infrastructure. It also supplies technical assistance and services;

o RIBS deals with the reorganization of enterprises which operate in the agro-industrial sector.

o It carries out projects, and establishes cooperative societies, consortiums and territorial and economic institutions to assist existing companies and also to grant funds and contributions to agricultural societies;

o Società di Promozione Industriale (The Society of Industrial Promotion) deals with the promotion and development of entrepreneurial activity, particularly in the iron and steel areas, by offering all kinds of assistance, both to entrepreneurs and societies, to facilitate the installing, organization and management of entrepreneurial activities. All this is done by supplying services and techno-managerial consultancy, participating in the company's capital risk and, in some regions, through participation in BIC which manages company incubators;

o Istituto di Promozione Industriale (Institution of Industrial Promotion) is the agency which specializes in promotion and technical consultancy in the field of regional industrial policies, paying particular attention to promotion in the depressed areas.

In January 1999, the Government, with the purpose of putting some order between all these organizations, set up a society called "Sviluppo Italia" in which by the end of 1999 the last five societies mentioned above were incorporated and will have three basic tasks: merchant banking, the promotion of entrepreneurial activities taken up by young people and also attracting industrial initiatives from abroad.

The following institutions promote SMEs on a regional level:

o Agenzie di Sviluppo Locale e Finanziarie (Local Development and Funding Agencies), which normally manage programmes and regional resources in favour of SMEs present on the regional territory;
o Business Innovation Centres, which are promoted by the European Union, and also local partners, which assist enterprises set up by young people and also innovative enterprises which have development programmes;
o Relay Centres, which are promoted by the European Union and the Ministry of Research.

These centres carry out assistance and follow-up activities regarding the transfer of the new technologies of the big firms and also for university research on SMEs;

o Scientific and Technological Parks, which, similar to the Relay Centres, favour technological transfer and also deal with research and technological research themselves;
o Gruppi di Azione Locale (Local Action Groups), which are promoted by the European Union and local partners. These groups carry out assistance and follow-up activities for enterprises situated in the internal areas of the region - areas which are particularly disadvantaged and suffer from a heavy demographic decline, above all in the field of agriculture and tourism.

There is a tightly knit network of both organizations and tools which are able to help and finance entrepreneurs. However, it is obvious how difficult it is for the entrepreneurs to find the best balance between the various institutions and tools to use for the start-up of their initiatives.

Generally speaking, an entrepreneur is heavily oriented towards his/her product and is not on very familiar terms with the supporting tools for his/her activity, so that is it vital that the various Governments should set up "orientative structures" which would allow entrepreneurs to combine their initiatives with the facilitation tools, aiming at utilising the resources available in the best possible way.

The incubator must be an interpreter and also give an answer to numerous problems, such as:

o the incapacity of the market to create enterprises. New entrepreneurs are hindered by entry barriers such as the high fixed costs in the manufacturing sector, a lack of information and suitable financial means and the sheer impossibility of carrying out training through mechanisms of communicating experiences;
o the need to modify the nature of the local economy or create additional employment after period of productive recession;
o the hope of creating a strongly vocational space for technological innovation;
o the possibility of offering an entrepreneurial opportunity for socially weak persons such as: women, young people, the unemployed, immigrants and so on.

It is obvious that this kind of activity cannot be invented in a short time and cannot give immediate answers. Moreover, this is not really an entrepreneurial activity, because the purpose is to reach budget levelling at the end of the year. It is therefore obvious that the shareholders in the society of the incubator cannot be entrepreneurs who wish to gain profits from this activity.

The partners of the incubator should be representative of a mixture of private and public interests. The mission of the incubator must be officially recognized as a mission of public interest and for this reason, financed. On the other hand, the returns are in terms of job creation and well-being, which are undoubtedly the main problem Public Administrations have.

The society must be mostly composed of public partners, who must guarantee the safeguarding of both local and public interests and, also have a vision which allows the management of the structure enough time to develop the strategies of the incubator.

Private partners, when they are involved, must guarantee efficiency, a managerial approach and a network of relations with the business world. They must be chosen with great care and must guarantee that they will not use the entrepreneurs' own ideas to develop up their businesses. Generally speaking, private partners are represented by:

o Banks and financial companies. Banks are always on the hunt for good business so the singling-out of an enterprise with good growth potential helps to sell their own financial products and services;

o Insurance companies and pension funds. They can activate the investments, it improves their image and in many countries these investments are tax-free;

o Large companies. Large companies are interested in developing this activity because in the worst case, they use these tools to expel their workforce by means of spin-off processes and out- placement. In the best of cases, these companies are interested in the new technologies developed inside the incubator.

Kyrgyzstan

The economic environment in Kyrgyzstan emphasizes the freedom of entrepreneurship and the development of the private sector through programmes and finance schemes. In addition, the

country has a high level of education and skilled personnel. The socio-psychological environment encompasses a favourable public atmosphere and an institutional structure, as well as a supporting infrastructure for SMEs, including consulting services and access to finance.

Latvia

The past three to four years of experience in the establishment and management of structures to support innovative businesses in Latvia has shown that there is a need to unite the efforts in this field. One of the tasks has been the need to increase awareness of the economic and social impact of such services at different governmental and non-governmental institutions and organizations. On the other hand, there is no legislative act or government policy concerning technology parks, centres and business incubators nor innovative businesses, based on which a national strategy could be developed.

The Latvian Association of Technological Parks, Centres and Business Incubators (LTICA) was established in September 1996. The founders were the representatives of three technology centres and parks as legal persons and some individuals as physical persons. In terms of its legal status the LTICA is a public organization with the following objectives:

o ?to establish links among all the business support structures in Latvia;

o to raise the level of qualification of its members;

o to represent and to protect the interests of the members;

o to create an information network to support technology-oriented SMEs;

o to promote the establishment of new business support structures;

o to support the transfer of technology and innovation;

o to create and maintain regional and international contacts;

o to co-operate with non-governmental and local authorities, science and research centres;

o to increase public awareness about LTICA and the activities of its member.

Republic of Moldova

One of the objectives of future business incubators is to promote the clustering of and cooperation among small and medium-sized enterprises. The large necessity for business incubators is felt in connection with the fact that many newly created enterprises do not have sufficient start-up capital and enterprise practice.

Poland

Business incubators and innovation centres are created mainly by local authorities and communities such as city councils, chambers of commerce and industrial and regional development agencies, as well as different foundations and associations for local development. Such local initiatives are supported by central institutions and, in particular, the Ministry of Labour and Social Policy, the Ministry of Economy, the Polish Foundation for Small and Medium Enterprise Promotion and Development and the Polish Agency for Regional Development.

The role and tasks of the Polish Association

of Business and Innovation Centres, established in 1992 can be characterized as:

- o development of an information system;
- o organization of meetings, lectures, training, consultations, conferences, symposia, competitions and conventions;
- o publishing information and training materials, as well as initiating the development of publications;
- o cooperation with other domestic and foreign organizations and institutions that conform to the Association's goals;
- o inspiring business research, innovation and local development;
- o cooperation with local and central authorities as well as with science and research centres.

The work of the Association and its members has resulted in:

- o nine annual conferences of Polish business incubators;
- o three conferences focused on technology and entrepreneurship;
- o eight manuals for business incubators;
- o dozens of presentations at conferences in Poland and abroad;
- o training courses arranged for business incubators and managers from Poland, Russia, Ukraine, Belarus, Uzbekistan;
- o training courses for Polish managers of Business and Innovation Centres in Germany, France, the United Kingdom and the United States of America;
- o a newsletter;
- o programmes for infrastructure development for business and innovation in Poland;
- o a cooperation network with governmental and central institutions in Poland.

Although not financed by the Government, the Association enjoys the support and confidence of governmental institutions. For example, the recent Task Force on Commercialization of Technology at the Ministry of Industry and Trade was chaired by and consisted mostly of members of the Association.

Russian Federation

Transition to the market economy in Russia goes along with such sophisticated processes as privatization of large public enterprises, and the formation of the layer of entrepreneurs and business infrastructure. Attention to the conditions of small business development at the Federal level had been quite limited due to preference for the large and medium-sized business problems.

During its first steps small business in Russia had the essential number of qualified and educated specialists but who had had no training and experience for market economy realities. The situation has started to change but there are still a lot of obstacles to overcome.

The legal base for small business until now continues to have a lot of strong contradictions, the elimination of which is indispensable for further business development. The taxation system does not provide any special benefits to small enterprises. Financial support to small businesses faces serious bureaucratic barriers, requested collaterals for borrowed assets sometimes are higher than needed loan amounts, which makes it inaccessible for the majority of entrepreneurs.

In terms of training there is a system of schools nowadays formed in Russia to train and retrain personnel for the small business sector. These schools and institutions adopt for the specifics of small business and provide short-term hands-on solutions for the problems that arise in everyday entrepreneurial practice. One of the examples is a network of business-training centres of the Morozov project that have been created in over 70 regions of Russia. These centres have a wide range of training programmes on different aspects of preparation for the entrepreneurial activity.

In terms of production space, business incubators provide start-up enterprises with equipped space for their activity. Business incubators themselves are often organized at the premises of large enterprises that had turned out to be ineffective in the conditions of the market economy. This explains the large diversity in reconstruction costs, which depend on the amount of space, initial conditions of the premises etc. and usually vary between USD 10,000 and 80,000.

Many incubators are created at big enterprises around which the economy of the cities and regions had been built. Under the market conditions business incubators assist regional economies in building new infrastructure and help to diversify and reorient to the new needs. Such incubators act in former military settlements, mining centres etc.

Business incubators in Russia are financed by governmental structures, foreign investors, federal and regional small business support funds. In many cases participation of State structures is in providing space or technological equipment.

Many incubators, besides basic office and training services, provide financial support to the incubated businesses. Such tools as credit unions, micro crediting, equipment leasing has shown prevalence and high effectiveness. Loan amounts from credit unions usually do not exceed $ 1,000 and this kind of financial assistance is subject to the lowest taxation rates. In micro crediting programmes credit amounts are about $ 10,000 and to get a credit an entrepreneur is supposed to develop a business plan and prove its efficacy. Another tool that proves to be effective in small business support in Russia is equipment leasing. Correctly organized, this method shows 100% return rate.

Governmental and commercial banks participate in small business support processes by providing credits and loans. However, to get a bank loan an enterprise must provide a collateral of liquid assets for the amount over the requested loan. Most of the enterprises do not have such assets. Interest rates of commercial banks are usually higher than the Central Bank rate, and are not affordable for the small businesses.

As to innovations support, there are specialized governmental fund organized to provide loans on preferential terms for innovative enterprises. Foundations that support innovative or priority-driven businesses are created in the majority of the regions of the Russian Federation.

Sweden

No incubator stands totally alone. Most of the Swedish initiatives are linked to a university, a Science/Technology Park or both. If the incubator is located in close proximity to the university and to other technology-related companies, then its tenants can benefit from the powerful and diverse competencies surrounding them. Normally there is also a strong support and interest from the local and regional authorities and government-financed development organisations.

It is up to the incubator staff to provide their tenants with an optimal business environment by interacting with professional consultants and other companies/organisations. Highly qualified persons in business development as well as people representing business opportunities have to be found and "invited" to be a part of the incubator network.

Swedish incubators initiate development programmes, which include helping the start-ups to develop in the right direction. We also encourage mentors—senior entrepreneurs—to provide advice and support. They are very often open-minded and helpful, in spite of the fact that they are helping a possible future competitor.

Larger companies, local and multinational, located near the incubator, contribute significantly to the start-up's success by doing business with them—especially in the field of software development. The anchor tenants in the parks tend to feel and express some kind of responsibility towards the start-ups, often "helping" them by hiring them in as consultants, testing new products, and even financing some research and development.

Turkey

In order to ensure adequate conditions and a professional environment, the Government of Turkey has defined the following key requirements for an incubator:

o terms of reference and conditions for transferring funds to the incubator need to be in place and a business plan presented;
o the availability of funds (in accordance with the annual budget) needs to be published and awareness raised in the community and among the stakeholders;
o a managing (parent) organization needs to be selected and assigned;
o the financing organization needs to make available the funds for the period as specified in the approved business plan;
o the performance of the incubator needs to be properly monitored and evaluated.

Uzbekistan

Within the framework of a UNDP project, a three-tier system was created with the participation of the State Committee for Management of State Property and Entrepreneurship Support of the Republic of Uzbekistan and the UNDP Office in Uzbekistan. As the financiers of the Project, these organizations determine its strategy and the main development priorities.

A Coordinating Committee (CC) of business incubators provides policy guidance, conceptual recommendations on the relation of business incubators with the general economic transformations in the country.

The Republican Business Incubator (RBI) and Project Support Unit consists of national and technical experts selected by the United Nations through a competition. They are responsible for the coordination of business incubators, distribution of financial and material resources and provision of methodological, organizational and technical support and consulting to business incubators.

The board and the management of the business incubators are responsible for the day-to-day operations and the development of concrete entrepreneurial activity directions in regions. The following directions are the most important for the further development of the business incubators system in Uzbekistan.

Enhancing the efficiency of business incubators: In this context, the introduction of a thorough tenant selection system and the expansion of services rendered by the business incubators (particularly, consulting on investment pro

grammes), as well as an intensive incubation of the tenant during the 1.5-2 year term, are currently among the most important development issues.

Another important goal is the financial sustainability of the incubators. Within the following one to two years, a stable and functional network of business incubators needs to be developed. According to some international estimates, 17 out of the 20 newly created incubators are potentially successful. To this end, the work plans have to be carefully designed. Since the beginning, all business incubators have been self-supporting and self-financing. However, the following measures should be undertaken:

- o the material and technical basis of incubators (office equipment, vehicles) need to be further strengthened to allow them to implement tasks more efficiently;
- o the level of qualification of the managers and personnel of the incubators needs to be raised, including exposure to some foreign experience as well;
- o the legal status of the business incubators needs to be changed, since the majority have been operating as a limited liability company

in which the Government has the controlling block of shares. The Republican Business Incubator, which is in charge of the overall development work, operates as a small enterprise with 100% of the shares belonging to the Government. To make the project more attractive for potential donors and investors, a business incubator association as a coordinating agency in the form of a non-governmental organization should be created.

PART II

CURRENT SITUATION

CHAPTER 5

SERVICES PROVIDED BY A BUSINESS INCUBATOR

Business incubators usually involve premises (real estate) where national or local Governments, municipalities, or groups of large-scale enterprises provide on-site workshop office and administrative services, and assistance in various areas such as technical support services, access to financing, counselling, marketing, access to equipment, and management assistance. The range of services available at the different kinds of institution varies greatly. However, in most countries, the services may cover a combination of the services listed below:

o   Physical infrastructure includes offices or workshop space on an affordable basis. Having a registered business place is the first essential step in starting one's business;

o   Secretarial services are provided for newly established small enterprises along with access to a mailbox, libraries and related services;

o   Telecommunications and information technology services usually include access to telephone, telefax, e-mail, and the Internet;

o   Business planning, assistance, resources, counselling services as one of the main tasks of a business incubator is to help make a business plan and advise on bookkeeping and filling in tax forms;

o   Advertising and marketing services such as the provision of lists of potential suppliers, businesses, potential investors, and distributors;

o   Financial advice services advising businesses on their funding and investments, as well as on their daily financial transactions;

o   Training services providing insight into the principles of market economy, as well as upgraded professional and technical skills;

o   Know-how services may be needed to help the tenants through the legal processes linked to the use of licences and know-how;

o   Network services are very important at a business incubator, in particular in a virtual business incubator, providing links and relationships with other organizations that can promote and sustain the interests of its client businesses;

o   Industrial infrastructure including roads, water, electricity, telecommunication, buildings and industrial machines can be provided. This is most common in technoparks;

o   Aftercare services after the incubation period. Successful companies are financially viable and free-standing when they leave the incubator, usually after two to three years;

o   Security services particularly for companies dealing with intellectual property, hi-tech products etc. risk being targets of industrial espionage - both physical in situ as well as hackers on the Internet. In addition, the risk of "ordinary" burglaries or thefts may be very high in some countries or certain areas or cities. An incubator can provide physical security services much more cheaply than an individual company could and also access to the latest systems of computer and related security that the companies alone might not be able to acquire.

The range of services, however, varies widely in different countries due to different traditions, financing models.

SPICE Group

The SPICE Group has identified the following areas where services should be rendered:

o   start-up advisory (business planning) and company development consulting;
o   letting of appropriate office, laboratory and/ or production space (below market rents, favourable terms);
o   technical and organizational services for young (innovative) enterprises (e.g. secretarial, conference facilities, telecommunication);
o   innovation- and technology-oriented services (technology transfer), as well as training and information;

o financial services.

In addition to the above basic set of services, an incubator can offer a wide range of technology and business community related services, such as:
o international innovation- and technology-oriented services (technology transfer), as well as training and access to information;
o market-oriented services (access to information, training, contacts, representation);
o location in the future market in a flexible manner according to the needs of foreign partners;
o local, regional, national and global networking, technical and human.

Bulgaria

High Technology Parks are envisaged to be legal entities, which manage and administrate one or more separate local areas including buildings and adjacent infrastructure with the objective of pursuing high technology activities. The parks support activities through:

o the pursuit of R&D for the development of high technologies in areas where individual enterprises cannot or would hardly obtain profit working on their own;
o the acquisition of up-to-date technologies (patented and non-patented inventions, licences, know-how, trade marks), machines and equipment;
o related logistic services and services related to them; services in the field of law, management, accounting, trade activities, market research and other business services directly concerned with high technologies in the country;
o vocational training and retraining in the high technologies; training of bachelor and master graduates through involving them in activities within the park;
o technical consultations and analyses for an entry to the markets.

An incubator's mission within a park is to actively help newly emerging hi-tech companies to survive and develop in the initial period when they are most vulnerable by:
o stimulating entrepreneurship and innovations in technologically oriented production;

o facilitating technological and financial evaluation of projects and developing R&D plans and business plans, and providing direct and indirect professional manager assistance;
o helping them?to gain access to investment capital and commercialize products;
o facilitating information and contacts with different government and international programmes, participation in international exhibitions, fairs etc.;
o offering flexible leasing schemes for workspace, normally with an extension potential and shared infrastructure, such as joint use of office services and access to equipment.

Croatia

Upon entering the incubator, an entrepreneur is eligible for a number of benefits. First of all, help will be given in the formulation of business plans and in the choice and realization of the organizational form of business. The entrepreneur can occupy business premises free of charge for the first year, but even later (throughout the stay in the incubator) the rent is moderate. The occupants are free to use the administrative and technical facilities of the incubator (telephone, telex, PC, photocopier, etc.) as well as the services of a business secretary. A particular advantage for the tenants of the incubator is the availability of counselling services.

The network centre of different incubators has made it possible to develop a system of business incubators and a data bank that will allow:
o exchange of information;
o entry into new markets;
o the creation of partnerships and new business relationships.

In addition to standard services of business incubators, technology centres provide the following services:
o search for strategic partners;
o preparation of business projects;
o preparation of feasibility studies;
o access to specialized software for investment projects (developed by the centre in Split and available only in Split);
o access to conference rooms.

Czech Republic

Business incubators in the Czech Republic are a local or regional institutions capable of offering, under beneficial conditions and terms for its clients, i.e. small medium-sized privately owned enterprises, a full and complete range of services focused on industrial innovations and supportive services:

o business and specialist advisory services;
o experience in assistance and services provided to emerging entrepreneurs;
o team of skilled and capable expert.

In addition to support for rent, operating expenses (electricity, water, etc.) and other necessary rent-related services, which are specified exactly in the agreement, the Business incubator may render other services, including:

o research and evaluation of emerging businesses;
o assistance and support to business innovation;
o business education and training;
o assistance and support to business plans;
o business incubators can also support technology centre activities, such as support SMEs to get established in the international market and create conditions for their prosperity.

Advisory services include:
o consultations and assistance to prepare a business plan;
o cooperation and assistance in the preparation of innovation processes;
o support to regional and cross border cooperation;
o support to access to the common market;
o organization of contacts and technology transfer;
o enhancing partner relationships among entrepreneurs;
o financial and organizational advisory services;
o organization of meetings and seminars.

Five science and technology parks and BICs have been internationally accredited by the European Business and Innovation Network, EBN. These units cooperate closely with different universities or research institutes of the Academy of Science of the Czech Republic. Some activity services of these units are eligible for the Phare support scheme administered by the Business Development Agency of Ministry of Industry and Trade. Some of these units also offer special services, such as dissemination of information about the 5th framework programme of the European Community for research, technological development and demonstration (RTD). Such advisory services are particularly useful for the spin-offs from universities and research institutes.

Estonia

The Tartu Science Park (TSP) offers services for the tenant companies, supports the launch of new R&D-based businesses, administers and maintains the TSP buildings and territory. The services offered to the companies by the science park include:

o low rents (3 - 4 DM per m2);
o communication lines (phones, fax, e-mail, Internet);
o assistance in finding credits and technical aid;
o dissemination of company information, help in finding relevant research or business partners;
o issuing the monthly TSP News Bulletin, arrangement of publications;
o organization of conferences, seminars, exhibitions, etc. or of attending these;
o equipped conference and meetings room, PC workplaces;
o photocopying, secretarial services, help with keeping international correspondence;
o maintenance of electricity, heating, water supply
o and waste removal systems, security of the site bar and sauna, organization of social events.

The companies can also benefit from participating in international networks that the park is involved in, including the International Association of Science Parks, the ICECE - Innovation Centres in Eastern and Central Europe and the Baltic Association of Science/Technology Parks and Innovation Centres.

The activity also involves improvement of infrastructure and services of the incubation centre and direction of its service network towards the target regions in order to support innovative SMEs and incubation/innovation institutions there by transferring the experience gained in training, counselling, application of new technologies, etc.

Finland

The average size of a Finnish business incubator is approx. 1,000 m2. Two thirds of all incubators have a full-time manager and the average number of employees is 2.6. The average annual operating expenses of a business incubator amount to US $ 200 000. A typical business incubator has 10-20 enterprises in incubation at a time.

On the other hand, there are incubators of a markedly bigger size. The biggest, the Otaniemi Science Park Ltd., consists of more than 100 enterprises. The operation of the whole Innopoli group, which offers its services even to technology companies other than those in incubation, involves about 220 enterprises or units, which have about 1,200 employees.

The supply of services provided by Finnish business incubators can be divided into the following groups: premises and equipment, office services, specialist services and financial services.

The basic supply of services provided by an incubator comprises office premises, conference rooms, as well as rest rooms and other facilities for the staff. Laboratory premises, rooms for video conferences and storage space, may complete these. All incubators do not, however, rent premises to enterprises or they rent premises only to some enterprises, allowing each enterprise establish itself in the environment best suited to its operations. However, in the definition of business incubators used by the EU, for instance, the term "business incubator" is used for enterprises operating under the same roof, and, therefore, this network form of incubation deviates from the definition above.

The basic equipment comprises copying machines, faxes and Internet connections. Typical services provided by an incubator are data processing and printing services. Among the office services available, enterprises in incubation usually have access to a telephone exchange, as well as mailing, secretarial and reception services. A common service is also joint meetings of entrepreneurs.

The following are some of the specialist services normally available for enterprises in incubation: managerial services; managerial consultancy; development of business operations; evaluation of new products and assistance in product development. Other services, such as the development of human resources, information and

communications, transfer of technology, export counselling, patents, taxation, accounting and legal services, are also provided by an incubator. Using external contractual services through the cooperative network at the incubator's disposal makes access to these services possible, for instance.

Financial services often include assistance in financial arrangements. The customers of a business incubator are unde certain circumstances eligible for public aid. The granted by the Government's regional development organization for covering the costs at the initial stage, and risk credits granted by a special finance company providing finance for SMEs. In addition to financing provided by banks, possible sources of finance among venture capital companies are especially local companies or the local seed financing system.

Georgia

Incubators must develop services, equipment, and management assistance to serve the targeted audience. An incubator encourages foreign investment, both financial and technological. An incubator also offers a range of services. For instance, the SEMA Project at the "Electroaparati" provides the following services:

o market research;
o assistance in drafting a business plan, including profit and loss and balance sheets;
o assistance in reducing unit costs through innovative design, purchasing, and construction methods;
o architectural design for projects;
o contacts with real estate agents, advertising agencies, and insurance companies;
o basic facilities, such as natural gas line and landscaping;
o assistance in the search for low-cost financing.

Complementary programmes may support the export of locally manufactured goods. These programmes may include components such as design and quality standards.

Germany

Differences between business incubators are reflected in more specialization and/or additional services offered to the tenant firms as well as to external clients rather than being differences in basic services (rooms for lease, start-up consulting, secretarial services). The key services of business incubators include:

- o start-up advisory (business planning) and company development consulting;
- o technical and organizational services for young (innovative) enterprises (e.g. secretariat, conference facilities, telecommunication, computers, workshops);
- o flexible letting of appropriate office, laboratory and/or production space (sometimes, but not necessarily, below market rents, favourable terms).

Additional services may include:

- o innovation and technology-oriented services (technology - transfer);
- o training and information - not exclusively for tenant companies;
- o financing services (equity, "business angels", seed and venture capital);
- o (international) business contacts and cooperation;

Hungary

The entrepreneurs in the incubators operated by local enterprise agencies have access to the following services that need to be delivered timely in a flexible manner and at privileged prices:

- o office and production space;
- o office services (typing, copying, phone and fax, mailing services);
- o consultancy (financial, business management, etc.);
- o access to information (all the information possessed by the agency is quickly accessible for the enterprises);
- o education, training;
- o exhibitions and meetings with the business community (enterprises can participate in the events organized or promoted by the agency, but events can also be initiated in the incubators exhibition and conference rooms and restaurants);
- o promotion of access to financial resources (micro credit and other services, credits and guarantee funds intermediated by the local enterprise agency);
- o purchases and orders on behalf of the local enterprise agencies and the tenants.

The local enterprise agencies draft annually a revised business plan based on the agreed structure and budget as set out in the Terms of Reference provided by the experts of the Hungarian Foundation for Enterprise Promotion and the European Union. As a result, every enterprise agency carries out the following activities:

- o provision of micro credit for small-sized and start-up enterprises;
- o providing entrepreneurs with office and workshop space, which in practice meant the construction and support of incubator houses and industrial parks;
- o entrepreneur training and education, organising and promoting businessmen meetings;
- o consultancy and information provision for the members of the SME sector;
- o development of programmes aiming at enterprise and economy promotion in sub-contracting and/or by the agency itself.

Italy

The success of an incubator and BIC depends on the following factors:

- o high quality services;
- o the relationship between cost and efficiency;
- o high specialization of the various competencies to support this particular stage of the enterprise.

BIC and the incubator must become a natural meeting-point for all those who operate in the sphere of services and local development: banks, universities, associations and consultants, in order to make sure that all these services will be offered in an integrated and coordinated manner. The capacities of the assisted entrepreneurs will improve and costs of the enterprise reduced to a minimum during this phase. The services offered by the incubator can be divided into three large categories: basic services, facilities and advanced services.

Basic services

Maintenance. The incubator must be constantly adapted to the needs of the enterprises which come to it and also to the new needs of those already occupying it;

Cleaning. The incubator must be kept clean, both in the interests of the enterprises working inside it and in the inter ests of the structure itself;

Security. The incubator must be protected from intrusion by people from outside, but at the same time, it will be necessary to guarantee free access for the employees to their workplaces, paying attention to the fact that they are the only ones who can have access - no other person may do so. This particular type of activity, apart from the laws which normally regulate the construction of buildings, requires special attention. Normally, all industrial plants have been planned and adapted to the needs of the firms which utilize the systems over long periods of time. In the case of incubators, however, the firm which replaces the outgoing firm might not have the same needs. Therefore, it is necessary that the installations should not only be planned to answer different needs but should also be easily inspected, replaced and strengthened;

Maintenance of the outside area: (gardening and parking areas). It might seem to be exaggerating when dealing with this subject, but it is most important to emphasise the fact that the image of the incubator is absolutely indispensable, above all, for the enterprises which operate inside the incubator. It is also important to underline the fact that compared to a traditional firm, the parking areas must be much larger as the firms in an incubator are more numerous;

Canteen services. According to the size of the incubator and to make the incubator functional for the firms working there, it could be appropriate to organise a canteen inside it, a canteen which must also be capable of organising exhibitions and other events inside the incubator. One simple and efficient way of organizing this could be that of choosing a catering company or even promoting one;

Gas, water, telephone, electricity, heating, air conditioning, etc. The problem of consumption is basically tied up with the various types of use and flexibility. It must be possible to establish with certainty the consumption of each single enterprise. Moreover, it must be possible to adapt it every so often to the needs of the incoming firms which replace the outgoing ones;

Communication services including Internet and Intranet. It is most important that the incubator be equipped with the latest and most modern means of communication in order to allow the firms to work inside a network, both on a local level, but above all, on an international level;

Waste disposal. This is a rather important matter as it is necessary for the incubator to be equipped with waste disposal for the firms housed inside it. This will obviously be of different volume

for the pharmaceutical sector when compared to the electronic firms or the metallurgical ones.

Facilities

Reception. The reception desk is an extremely delicate service, as apart from answering the phone, the receptionist must control the hall and receive and screen the visitors for the various enterprises. At the same time the reception must be able to visualize access to the corridors leading to the rooms in which the equipment in common is housed;

A switchboard, telefax, telex and photocopying machine. Answering the phone is a very important function, particularly for a new firm, almost always of medium size. A personalized approach on the phone is really important. Messages have to be taken, phone calls made and appointments fixed on behalf of the various enterprises. Such an employee must be able to make phone calls and answer calls from abroad. So that rather than one secretary and a real reception, we have here an activity which requires the commitment of people with a veryhigh operative profile. The people who are committed to this function have to manage secretarial services such as the fax, telex, photocopying machine, etc.;

Meeting rooms. These are necessary for receiving people and holding internal meetings, thus avoiding having one's attention distracted from the daily routine. The halls should be of two kinds - a smaller one for gatherings of a limited number and a larger one for meetings, administrative committees and large meetings. These rooms are managed by the reception and must be booked in advance;

Conference rooms. These halls must be equipped to hold up to 100 people, both for conferences and for meetings. They must have a television set, a video recorder, a blackboard, monitors, videoconferences, etc.;

Showrooms. The hall of the incubator must be large enough to house important meetings and special events such us the presentation of a new firm or a new product. It must also contain a permanent display of the products of all the firms present in the incubator.

Advanced services

The short list which follows includes the typical services supplied by BIC, which can also be supplied without the incubator:

Business plan. This is an extremely important task as there are many people who have good ideas but do not know how to put them into action. They must therefore be helped to make a market assessment, assess the costs and sales proceeds, the financial necessities, the distribution networks and so on;

Management control. After management start-up it is necessary to help the entrepreneurship to formulate and utilize a control system;

Marketing assistance. Generally speaking, the new entrepreneur knows his/her product thoroughly, but hardly ever has a knowledge of the market and sales systems, so is not usually a good salesman. This problem gets even more complicated if the market is foreign;

Legal assistance. Most importantly during the initial phase, entrepreneurs tend to underestimate a whole series of problems which can then have legal consequences, and it is at this stage that they should be made aware of this factor. In any case, the right kind of professionalism must be available;

Centralized administration. Centralized bookkeeping and administrative management permits considerable financial savings plus better quality results. This activity could also be useful to BIC in order to find financing or partners for the assisted firms as BIC will know the company situation very well;

Partner research. BICs are part of a network which in turn is part of other local, national, and international networks, so that the research for partners becomes quite a simple matter. But it is not at all easy to get results because of the complexity of the work involved;

Financial services and seed capital. The enterprises going through the start-up phase often need financing and in any case the bringing-in of capital is always useful to accelerate the growth process of the enterprise;

Centralized bank data. There are various types, those which are useful for market and technological analyses, for patents and so on, and others for partner research, funding research and organizing meetings, events and demonstrations and displays;

The library. The library should be of the conventional kind and contain generally useful texts for all kinds of activities. The subscription for magazines should follow the same logic as it would be practically impossible to fill a library with specialized material in all sectors.

Kyrgyzstan

In Kyrgyzstan the services provided to the client companies can be presented under the headings:

Premises for enterprises
- o premises for enterprise administration;
- o premises for joint use of several companies (training classes, conference rooms, rooms for meetings, space for officeequipment, storage rooms).

Office services
- o access to common office equipment;
- o secretarial services;
- o information services;
- o joint bookkeeping services;
- o telephones;
- o access to translators and interpreters, as appropriate;
- o assistance in negotiations;
- o advertising services;
- o publication and related services;
- o security and cleaning services;
- o furnishing services.

Consulting and training
- o assistance in preparing business plans and financial applications;
- o venture capital of the incubator available for the enterprises;
- o assistance in finding access to financial resources;
- o financial guarantees for the enterprises.

Provision of business contacts
- o assistance in establishing contacts with business communities

Republic of Moldova

Future business incubators will provide the following services by themselves or attracting respective businesses:
- o leasing of equipment and renting of space and premises at reasonable prices, including

the supply of electricity, heating, water, internal telecommunications, internal transportation, loading/unloading works, equipment repairing, cleaning and lift service etc.;

o access to telephone, fax, e-mail and the Internet;

o access to finance and insurance, including venture and seed capital and other financial resources;

o access to training for managers and qualified employees;

o assistance in the preparation of business plans, qualified management consulting, book-keeping services, auditing;

o advertising and marketing services (marketing research, benchmarking);

o counselling on the use of licensing, patents and know-how;

o technical licensing and standardization;

o CAD/CAM technologies;

o organization of seminars and meetings with the business community and banks, government and local authorities and other organizations. Assistance in setting contacts with local authorities;

o secretarial services, including typing, printing, copying, binding and translations of documents;

o security services: guards and fire protection;

o social services, including canteens, restaurants and bars, fitness-centres and sauna.

Poland

The business and innovation centres aim at solving local economic and social problems by:

o training entrepreneurs in how to start a business and develop an enterprise in a free market economy;

o identifying and evaluating new business projects and providing technical, economic, financial, legal and other forms of consulting, assisting in acquiring access to financing for the business projects and making acquisition of capital easier;

o assisting in business planning, technology transfer, and in getting access to idle production room providing floor for new businesses.

The following types of centre provide all the above-mentioned services: business incubators, business and innovation centres and science and technology parks, while business support centres, small business development centres and small business institutes and clubs do not provide premises.

Russian Federation

A business incubator usually provides various combinations of the following services, aimed at creation of favorable conditions for small business development:

o Space and basic services:
  - Comfortable office and production premises and their maintenance
  - Meeting rooms and other facilities (warehouses, conference rooms, café etc.)
  - Security services
  - Secretarial services
  - Information services
  - Marketing services
  - Attraction of industry experts to assist small businesses
  - Attraction of business experts to assist small businesses
  - Legal, accounting, audit and other services

o Training and consulting:
  - Training courses on business planning, marketing, management and other issues
  - Short-term seminars on urgent questions
  - Consulting and mentoring services
  - Education facilities (business library, training classes, computers etc.)
  - Assistance in business-plans creation and analysis

o Financial support:
  - Guarantee funds
  - Equipment leasing
  - Micro-crediting
  - Investments, venture financing
  - Favorable payment terms for business incubator's services
  - Promotion for outside financing

o Psychological support:
  - Creation of positive business atmosphere
  - Consulting of psychologists (problem solving, personnel issues, stress reduction)
  - Interest in clients' problems

Each incubator individually offers a final set of services, depending on the need of its target clients and environmental specific.

Slovakia

In addition to premises, the companies are provided with services such as business counselling, assistance in searching of financial resources, office services (copy, fax, Internet, e-mail, filing, etc.), assistance in establishing both national and international business contacts, and help to solve problems in human resources management, marketing, etc.

Slovenia

In fulfilling its mission, the Technology Park in Ljubljana provides support to technology companies by incorporating them into a favourable environment and assisting them in developing new technologies, products and services and in accessing the marketplace. The working methods ensure less risk and greater effect, subsidization of operations and the optimal use of invested funds. In addition the mission of the Technology Park comprises:

- o generating motivation and a climate for the development of businesses based on in-house skills;
- o promoting self-employment as a modern trend within society;
- o creating a positive image of the entrepreneur;
- o providing in-depth information to business people;
- o creating new jobs in the region;
- o assisting the conversion of regional potential into commercial enterprises;
- o giving the region's hi-tech enterprise a profile in the markets through foreign partners and international networks of links.

Business infrastructure includes the organization and carrying out of support activities for the members and other users according to the following categories of services:

Advertising, marketing
- o design of advertising materials;
- o joint participation in domestic and inter national fairs;
- o public relations;
- o market research;
- o use of databases;
- o exhibitions and presentations within the promotion centre.

Training, professional meetings
- o seminars;
- o thematic workshops;
- o conferences;
- o meetings with representatives of different ministries and other domestic or foreign institutions.

Information
- o ISDN connections;
- o ccess to the Internet;
- o stock exchanges;
- o various databases;
- o COBISS electronic library.

Business consultancy
- o free advice on a daily basis;
- o specialists' business advice;
- o business advice related to the management of knowledge, finance, personnel, etc.

Transfer of technology
- o international cooperation and transfer of knowledge;
- o transfer of technology between the University and carriers of entrepreneurial programmes;
- o international promotional events;
- o managing of the local business centre for the promotion of entrepreneurship and transfer of technology within seven municipalities;
- o support to innovation technologies and patents.

Sweden

Incubator activities can be very different from one location to another, but all incubators are guided by the basic premise that they should provide as much assistance as possible to bring a start-up business to a certain level of performance and success. The staff organise seminars and meetings to provide entrepreneurs with information related to business planning, finance, marketing, regulatory and tax issues, management, and overall business development. Many of these seminars will be conducted by individuals or agencies in the larger incubator network.

Within the incubator network, there are organisations that provide various levels of seed capital start-ups. Swedepark, the national Swedish organisation for Science and Technology Parks one programme offers seed money for start-ups, as do the Swedish National Board for Industrial and Technical Development (NUTEK), ALMI, and the Technology Bridge Foundation (regional development organisations).

One of the most important services offered to both pre-incubator and incubator tenants is entrepreneurship training. Often organised by universities together with senior entrepreneurs, these initiatives have proven extremely successful by giving the participants a solid platform in entrepreneurship and in business management and organisation. Universities can also provide incubator tenants with a qualified work force and access to academic consultation and research.

Infrastructure is also extremely important. Start-ups need to receive as much value as possible for the money they spend. Low-cost space gives a new company the opportunity to put any money they may have into developing the business. Once they see a return on their investments, they can afford higher rents.
All companies today, whether established or start-up, need high-speed, broadband digital networks and connection to the Internet.

Swedish incubators are to a large extent influenced by the local and regional physical and economic environment, as are the Science Parks. None of them looks or operates exactly the same, although they share similar objectives.

Uzbekistan

Business incubators can successfully implement innovative projects. Consequently, measures are required on how to introduce local technologies and development into production. These services are coordinated with the appropriate agencies and structures including the Committee for State Property of Republic of Uzbekistan, the State Committee for Science and Technology, banks, etc.

Attracting investment. Although this is being fairly successfully carried out by the business incubators already, it is important to consolidate their efforts to attract foreign investment including currency credits, direct investment for joint ventures and grants from international organizations. Activities in this direction can also improve the financial situation of the incubator owing to commissions from their consulting activities;

Training of entrepreneurs. Business incubators are successfully involved in this sphere of activity, although implementing target programmes by incubators (coordinating with the local authorities and concerned organizations) can not only help incubators to carry out purposeful works but also contribute considerably to their achievement of financial sustainability. In this context, support of regional divisions by the Committee for State Property, the Chamber of Goods Producers and Entrepreneurs, as well as the Ministry of Labour could be extremely important;

CHAPTER 6

FORMS OF BUSINESS INCUBATOR

There is no standard legislation regarding business incubators. However, specific government policies on business incubators have often played an important role e.g. as regards regional development or the development of high technology industry. The goal needs to be an enabling environment by setting up institutions and providing incentives for enterprise creation and economic growth.

Business incubators as legal entities can often be established in the following organizational patterns:
- A non-profit business incubator running with the help of a community or an economic development foundation;
- ?A non-profit business incubator running with the help of a community or an economic development foundation;
- A private or for-profit incubator usually owned by venture and seed capital investment groups or real estate development partnerships;
- A joint effort of the local and central Government, a non-profit private organization. A partnership allows the incubator to take advantage of both the expertise of the private sector and the use of public funding;
- An affiliation of a university. The purpose of such a business incubator is to help in the development and transfer of new technology.

In some of the UN/ECE member countries the situation is as follows:

Azerbaijan

In Azerbaijan only university incubators started by the national Academy of Sciences can operate.

Bulgaria

Bulgaria's draft high technologies development strategy gives a leading position to high technology parks and for technological incubators as the implementation tools of government policies in the sector.

Croatia

The National Science and Research Programme 1996-1998 (Official Gazette 6/96) gives the definition of the National network of technology centres which serves as the official framework for establishing incubators for technology-based enterprises. The definition reads as follows: the National network of technology centres consists of a range of institutions directed towards development, transfer, introduction, application and/or financing of new technologies, and includes six basic institutional subjects:
- business innovation centres which operate outside university but in close cooperation with them;
- technology transfer centres which operate as "bridges" between university and industry;
- Financial institutions;
- forecasting and monitoring institutions;
- societies for innovation and engineering;
- other centres of excellence in technology.

Unlike technology centres, which are focused on supporting enterprises based on new, advanced or high technologies, business incubators are oriented to support all kinds of entrepreneurs regardless of the level of technology development.

There are no firmly defined criteria for the establishment of business incubators. Cofounders, usually local authorities of cities and counties, establish the criteria for founding and supporting the incubators under their responsibility.

As far as technology centres are concerned, the Ministry of Science and Technology sets up informal, but mandatory, criteria for establishing and supporting the centres, as follows:
- provision of a business plan for a future centre with the key elements of establishing which includes: co-founders, financial plan and resources, investments, premises, managers, development plans, etc.;
- mandatory participation of local authorities and universities/faculties as cofounders;
- provision of the money resources needed for the first year of functioning, with a financial plan for the future period;
- a manager who meets the criteria for

managing the centre according to the standards of foreign experienced business incubators;

o premises for entrepreneurs (at least 500 m2 at the beginning with the projection of their extension);

o provision of the mandatory services for entrepreneurs: rooms for leasing, offices, conference room, secretarial services, consulting in business, finance, technology, marketing, and legal matters.

The technology centres under the auspices of the Ministry of Science and Technology are:

o Centre of Technology Transfer, Zagreb, established in 1996 as a limited liability company with the support of MOST at the Faculty of Mechanical Engineering;

o Technology Centre Split, established in 1997 as a limited liability company with the support of MOST, Telecommunication centre in Split, County of Splitsko-Dalmatinska, and University of Split;

o Technology Innovation Centre, Rijeka, established in 1997 as a limited liability company with the support of MOST, University of Rijeka, County of Primorsko-goranska (and several companies on a small scale).

The incubators under the auspices of local authorities are:

o The Kon ar Technology park, Zagreb, established in 1994;

o The PORIN Business Incubator, Rijeka, established in 1996;

o The PINS Business Incubator, Skrad, established in 1997;

o The PLATIN Business Incubator, Cres/LoÜinj, established 1998.

All incubators are established as limited liability companies. They are mainly in public ownership. The owners of the Koncar, PORIN and PINS are the cities where the centres are located.

There is no simple incubator model that can be adopted. The business incubator should ideally be financed by the national, regional or local Government. Initial funding often comes from local or international project financing. Any type of business incubator can work efficiently, depending on the purpose of its establishment.

The oldest incubator in Rijeka is "Porin"

started in 1996. There are two new incubators in Pins and Platin. Their activities are connected with local Governments (Departments for Economy and Entrepreneurship) and through them with other organizations in the enterprise development system in Croatia.

Czech Republic

All forms of organizational patterns of businesincubators enumerated earlier in the introduction are present in the Czech Republic, too. The legal framework of their formation is different for each particular group. Sometimes, a drawback of a limited legal independence is compensated by better economic conditions resulting from a positive financial situation of a strategic partner. A list of science and technology parks and BICs in the Czech Republic is available on http://www.svtp.cz/stpmemb.htm.

Georgia

There is no legal definition of a business incubator, industrial zone and science park in Georgia, but the Government is determined to have one developed. Today, incubators can emerge to meet different business needs, such as:

o industrial subcontracting, supporting the development of new business as vendors. The features include quality control and programmes for production scheduling;

o individual business incubators have programmes specifically tailored to the needs of particular industrial products in sectors such as biotechnology, computer software, metal work, handicrafts, ceramics, and agro-business;

o university incubators specialize in supporting the development of businesses started by the faculty and the staff of the university, or are otherwise linked to the university.

Germany

In Germany the term innovation centre is used for the American "incubator". The innovation centres all offer rental space. This means the so called "incubators without walls" are not summarized under the term. This fact is related with the definition given above and aimed at making a difference between innovation centres on one hand and, on the other hand "business support centres" or "commercial real estate projects".

Physically innovation centres exist in all kinds of environment, e.g. in city centres and rural areas, in, near or far away from universities, as a separate building or a part of a building used for other commercial purposes as well, in old (renovated) industrial facilities or as a new building, in business/industry parks as well as in science/technology parks. In short: there is no "typical" innovation centre.

The most common legal form is a "limited company". Shareholders are usually economic development agencies and/or cities/municipalities. Quite common is the participation of chambers of commerce, banks and research institutions (universities). Less often private companies are to be found as shareholders. The recent development shows a growing interest of venture capital funds in participating or even fully owning and operating an innovation centre.

Hungary

Incubators are primarily operated by non-profit foundations or public organizations. However, some incubators operate as an affiliation of a university. In 19991, the Hungarian incubators established the National Association of Hungarian Incubators. This association provides professional assistance for the newly established incubator houses.

Kyrgyzstan

The management and organization of an incubator is an umbrella structure based on private personal ownership.

Republic of Moldova

It is expected that business incubators will be formed as a result of the reorganization of some industrial enterprises.

Russian Federation

The legislation of the Russian Federation does not provide any special legal form for a business incubator that would satisfy all the specifics of its activity, which often has to do with commercial actions for non-commercial purposes.

Incubator managers approach this issue proceeding from the requirements of the founders and the task of taxation minimization.

Among the legal forms often used for business incubators are the following:
o   Non-commercial partnerships;
o   Foundations and associations;
o   Non-state educational institutions;
o   Joint-stock companies;
o   Structural departments of state educational institutions.

The specific of the listed legal forms is stipulated in the Civil Code of the Russian Federation.

Non-commercial partnership is convenient for the business incubator because it allows to include both commercial and non-commercial structures in the circle of co-founders and provides flexible financial management and reporting systems.

Non-state educational institutions after licensing get exempted from Value Added Tax. Because most of the incubators provide educational and consulting services, funds saved on taxes can be uses for developing other kinds of services.

Foundations and associations allow accumulating funds for the activity stipulated by the charter.

Sweden

Because there is no specific legislation regarding incubators or parks, the forms vary. For example one can find:

o   Non-profit incubators - very often with basic funding from local or regional bodies,
o   For-profit incubators - often funded by real-estate companies or venture capitalists, or
o   Joint ventures between public and private money.

The university interest is seldom seen in terms of funding. Their contribution is through programmes and links to faculties, students, and research laboratories.

On the operational level Sweden has at least

two kinds of incubator: the pre-incubator and incubator (or "start-house" and "growth-house", as they sometimes are called). Pre-incubation is often limited to 12 months and often open only for those who have attended an entrepreneurship programme, this is a "test your idea in real life"-type of incubator. Tenants receive one or two small rooms at a low cost.

The regular incubator (growth-house) is for start-up companies that have come out of the start house, or spun out of a university or corporation. When the companies grow too big, they must leave the incubator system, but they often choose to stay in the park-environment in space available to larger companies.

CHAPTER 7

STRENGTHS AND WEAKNESSES OF BUSINESS INCUBATORS

Business incubation is a tool for enterprise development - an important one but nevertheless, a mere tool that needs to be used for the purposes set forth by the institution in question. It can be an incubator breeding new enterprises largely, or a science park or industrial zone, where the incubation services are included in a wider programme.

Depending on the type and purpose of the institution, the main benefits of a business incubator include the following:

o   it can become a long-term economic development tool for the community where it is located helping to diversify the economy, and increase tax revenue;
o   it can help change attitudes towards personal initiative, innovation, risk-taking and entrepreneurship;
o   it helps entrepreneurs to start their own businesses and gives them an advantage over new non-incubator firms;
o   it creates job opportunities;
o   it greatly increases the likelihood of survival of a new small ore medium-sized firm;
o   it allows the tenants to exchange information and discuss mutual commercial interests;
o   it helps retain individuals who would otherwise leave the area owing to the lack of job opportunities;
o   it helps rehabilitate and reuse existing buildings;
o   it helps enhance the community's image as a centre for innovation and entrepreneurship;
o   it encourages the development and transfer of new technology;
o   it promotes the clustering of SMEs, which helps overcome their biggest weaknesses – isolation and powerlessness– and raise their competitive potential through the emergence of linkages between firms providing economies of scale and scope;
o   it itself is a dynamic model of sustainable, efficient business;
o   it helps generate jobs and income beyond those directly employed and paid through the incubator's tenants. Thanks to the assistance

of the business incubator, the tenants are able to employ a larger workforce and increase their own revenues. This increase has a direct consequence in state revenue growth through the taxes an enterprise has to pay. The extra income means more capital that the local Government can contribute to the funding of business incubators.

Entrepreneurs criticize the business incubator for the following two most common constraints:
- o incubators help only a handful of firms;
- o incubators do not fully cover the operational costs, thereby obliging entrepreneurs to seek additional funding e.g. through special programmes.

Depending on their institutional set-up and operating environment, the strengths and weaknesses of the incubators may vary significantly:

SPICE Group

Different success factors influence the results of a business incubator, depending on its type and goals. Such factors may include:
- o the management and manager of the centre;
- o the advisory structure including the board of directors;
- o access to financing (seed, equity, venture);
- o existing networks and access to external support.

Azerbaijan

The principal strength of the future business incubator is the possibility of developing young ambitious non-oil companies and creating a favourable infrastructure for them. The major weakness is the lack of infrastructure for the transfer of various technologies.

Croatia

The strengths of the Croatian business incubators and technology parks are:
- o skilled and qualified management and personnel;
- o good cooperation with the regional research and development institutions;
- o good cooperation with the local industry; most of the incubated firms are growing successfully and are satisfied with the

conditions in the centres as well as with the services of the centres.

The most important problems regarding the management of the centres include:
- o although the cooperation with the local authorities and ministries is good there is a lot of space for continuous improvement;
- o the centres have limited premises for reaching the breakpoint of self-financing - the creation of the new jobs is not rewarded financially and some centres would need more spacious premises in order to be able to reach the break-even point;
- o the financial instruments are not always attractive for start-ups, there is a clear need for risk/seed capital which could be invested in tenant companies;
- o the modest growth in Croatian economy expected in year 2000 should enable better business environment for the tenant companies and the centres themselves;
- o there is a need to improve the analytical tools and methods for international market analyses.

Czech Republic

The system of business incubation as described in the introduction is operated in very different locations and under different conditions. However, the system has proved to be viable even under the modest external financial support. The most important weakness is a slow implementation of the system in some of the country's regions facing increasing sectoral unemployment, particularly in the northern parts of Bohemia and Moravia.

Georgia

One of the constraints in Georgia is the lack of infrastructure for the promotion of technology transfer. To this end, the development idea of the Centre for Enterprise Restructuring and Management Assistance (CERMA) is to create a business park in the "Electoaparati" plant in Tbilisi.

Germany

The most important strengths of innovation centres are:
- o a complex and comprehensive offer of all services needed for a start-up enterprise;

o the integration of different local/regional resources in a network stimulating innovation and economic development;

o the possibility of flexible adaptation (of the concept) to specific local needs and potentials - an innovation centre is a concrete response to local/regional needs;

o the continuous adaptation to the development of the region.

A weakness of innovation centres (in Germany) is the dominating influence of the public sector. The future development has to strengthen the entrepreneurial component of innovation centre management without losing the contact with and support of the public sector. After all, innovation centres play a major role in regional economic development promotion which is - in the German understanding - a public task.

Hungary

Based on the experience of Hungarian incubators, the keys to success are as follows:

o successful choice of premises: It is essential that the incubator itself has premises suited to its work. There need to be an area for the incubators administration as well as common areas for activities (seminars, negotiations, exhibitions, as appropriate given the services rendered). At the same time, the tenants need to have sufficient premises suited there particular line of business;

o Gradual development: the capacity and quality need to mach the demand. An incubator cannot operate if it is too big or too elaborate for the tenants. At the same time, quality should be higher than that of an average entrepreneur to keep the incubator attractive and also to create a certain status for the tenants. It is reasonable to start with a smaller investment because the demands of entrepreneurs are not easy to assess at the beginning;

o Early and successful choice of a director: the director should be involved in the design of the concept as this will increase his or her commitment;

o A comprehensive range of services: all services need to help the entrepreneurs. It is important also to consider advanced services such as business training, business meetings, exhibitions, consulting, provision of information, publications, access to micro-credit, resource coordination consulting, and initiating and managing development programmes;

o Special incubator atmosphere: it is important that the incubator not only be imposing on the outside, but the personal relationship between the staff and the tenants should also be advocating entrepreneurship and initiative;

o Appropriate choice of tenants: special care must be taken to avoid even the possibility of businesses disturbing one another. In fact, one should aim at selecting businesses that may even provide services to one another.

Threats may include the following:
o the minimal size needed for self-sustainability is 2,000 m2 rental area. A smaller size usually endangers self-sustainability;

o the investment and operational support needed for reaching the optimal size is indispensable. Lack of initial support is a threat to smooth operation.

Italy

University produces entrepreneurial subjects and ideas which are then put into the incubator. BIC assists the incubator by giving it all the services it needs and the Scientific Park does the same regarding the technological validation of an idea. The incubator is the internal area in which the neo-entrepreneur develops his own idea. Company incubators are considered as one of the tools for promoting employment through the creation of enterprises. In this sense it is quite obvious that an incubator is not by itself a guarantee for success, as incubators can flop just like any other business concern.

An analysis has found five main factors which can cause failure in an incubator:
o when no local partnership exists for the financing and management of the incubator;
o expecting positive results too quickly;
o bad choice of the executives;
o exaggeration of the actual role of the incubator;

o when the incubator is too expensive.

Republic of Moldova

A lack of experience in business incubation does not allow defining their strong and weak features. However, it is obvious that the Republic of Moldova's strengths in business incubation include the following:
o availability of essential industrial, personnel, administrative and technological potential;
o attractive conditions for SMEs in terms of low rents and prices for services;
o vailability of premises, facilities, and equipment is an extremely important factor in Moldova.

Moldova's weaknesses of business incubation include the following:
o limited support to enterprises;
o low level of entrepreneurship in the country;
o low level of investment into modernization and the development of enterprises;
o lack of legislative base;
o lack of financial and technical support from the Government.

Poland

Assistance programmes in Poland have usually been focusing on improving existing operations, incrementally changing processes, or introducing the essential concepts of free market economics. They seldom address the core determinants of technology development or transfer. Few assistance programmes have had to do with actual technology development. To this end, infrastructure is needed for promoting technology transfer.

It is essential for a business and innovation centre starting out to know what economic conditions it will address and who the target groups are. This is crucial not only for how the centre is arranged and managed but also for building and maintaining support among the community network. Making a business and innovation centre part of the local economic development process is vital in ensuring that the centre evolves to the point of adding value to the local economy. Sustainability of the project after external funding is completed is the most essential feature of any programme. In Poland, sustainability is defined as the interrelationship of three factors that impact on the future continuation of the initiative as follows:
o Financial: the ability to bring in new local sources of income on a continuous basis while managing to keep costs at an appropriate level;
o Institutional: the commitment to the project provided by an established organization that provides premises, low or no-cost resources and personnel. All these are necessary to give any project an image of strength and a long-term viability to those who choose to use its services;
o Managerial: the leadership capacity and project-related skills of those managing the project and their commitment to stay with the project and train others over time.

There are 10 basic premises of sustainability. In designing any externally funded project, Poland proposes the following criteria:
o Creating institutions versus providing programmes;
o The programme itself is not enough;
o Institutions have their own interests and incentives;
o Institutions must learn how to be "tough";
o Institutions must adopt a commercial approach;
o Institutions must be realistic and focused;
o Target groups must be incorporated in the institution's mission;
o Institutions should be professional and efficient;
o Institution must fit into local initiatives;
o People are the most valuable part of every institution.

The following factors are regarded as significant in innovation promotion and in the struggle against unemployment:
o appropriate government support;
o active regional policy;
o a modern system of education favouring continuing education and re-education;
o changes of mentality, particularly among the unemployed and persons threatened by unemployment;
o development of entrepreneurship;
o enhanced job finding services;
o dynamic economy stimulated by free and open markets.

Russian Federation

Among the strengths of Russian business incubators for the present moment the following features can be pointed out:
- o Acting business incubators have proved to be an effective tool for local economies development and job creation with minimum initial financial investments;
- o Economic effectiveness of a business incubator in the framework of a region is very high and initial costs are indirectly covered by taxes generated by the incubated enterprises within a year;
- o Business incubators perfectly fit in the newly developing market infrastructure in the regions, naturally support innovations and the whole process of business environment formation;
- o Business incubators in Russia function as structures that unite the interests of the emerging class of entrepreneurs and business owners;
- o Inside incubators the atmosphere of understanding of the importance and respect for business people and business activity in the countries with a market economy is being formed;
- o Business incubators are able to provide businesses with all the complex of necessary services at the right time and on attractive conditions;
- o Russian business incubators are able to attract for joint efforts a wide range of specialists of a very high professional level;
- o The number of business incubators in Russia is much lower than that needed, and therefore local administrations are interested in the creation of the new ones;
- o In the regions that used to have high level of specialization (mining regions, former military settlements etc.) business incubators help forming diversified market infrastructure and creating jobs.

Development of business incubators and small business in general are restrained by a number of factors, among which there are the following:
- o Non-stable political and economic situation in the country, absence of economic doctrine for market oriented development;
- o Legislation defaults on the part of small business support;
- o Absence of governmental policy for the small business development and forming support infrastructure;
- o Low level of business culture;
- o Sophisticated bureaucratic system of state control and management, certification, licensing etc. for the small business;
- o Impracticability of the current taxation system, absence of special conditions for developing small businesses;
- o Lack of information;
- o Absence of flexible system of financial support for small businesses and for the support institutions;
- o Low level of international cooperation in the area of technology transfer.

Slovenia

Investing and operating in enterprise zones can be important for improving companies' competitiveness. The effects are usually dependent on the conditions offered by the zone itself, as well as on the strategic partners residing in it. Some of the advantages include:

- o Low initial investment: cost of premises, infrastructure, construction, non-returnable funds, and tax relief;
- o Shorter start-up time for the investment: area planning, infrastructure, financial construction, available workforce, easy administrative processes;
- o Partnerships and cooperation: a defined volume of assured market share, growth with the environment or with a strategic partner, joint development ventures and market presence, achievement of higher price classes, acquisition of business information;
- o Reduced operating costs: economies of scale, common business functions, capacity utilization, reduced fixed operating expenses, good business infrastructure, and quality work force;
- o Logistics: rapid flow of products and services: reduced transportation, warehousing and manipulative costs, distribution to the consumer;
- o Transfer - acquisition of new technologies and expertise from a strategic partner, from joint development ventures;
- o Reduced operating costs due to benefits: taxes, customs duties, labour costs, levies, cheaper and better quality after sales service. Service, customer relations and feedback, publicity;

o Benefits arising from good relations with the surrounding environment: Joint resolution of environmental and development problems, upgraded skills of employees, area expansions, image of the company and identification of the environment with the company;

o The effects on the development of the region include increased buying power of the population, attractiveness for foreign investors and strengthening of own markets that can increase the quality of living.

In the following, some advantages and disadvantages of enterprise zones are discussed as they are viewed by different stakeholders:

o Advantages of enterprise zones from the State's perspective:
  - efficient instrument for accelerating economic development;
  - efficient instrument for attracting investors to certain areas;
  - contribution to greater efficiency and competitiveness of companies;
  - interaction of public and private interests;
  - transfer of foreign knowledge and experience;
  - possibility of combining various stimulating measures;
  - more efficient protection of the environment;
  - possibility of monitoring effects.

o Disadvantages of enterprise zones from the State's perspective:
  - unrealistic demands of local communities towards the State, to use this instrument in
  - inappropriate locations or unsuitability of the requested type of zone;
  - relatively high initial investment needed;
  - if there is no strategic partner, a lack of trained personnel and no appropriately represented enterprise interest, which would enable the long-term development of the zone (a demanding instrument, which should only be used selectively);
  - little experience in this area.

o Advantages of enterprise zones from the

local communities' perspective:
  - investors are attracted;
  - strengthening of local economy;
  - opening of new workplaces;
  - financial, informational and material flows are attracted to the area;
  - a regulated site for economic activities, which affects the appearance of the whole area;
  - development of service activities in the surroundings;
  - increased extent of state aid;
  - increased extent of original income.

o Disadvantages of enterprise zones from the local communities' perspective:
  - demands a full-time engagement by the local leadership;
  - relatively high initial investment;
  - a demanding project, which requires knowl
  - edge and experience;
  - potential environmental impact;
  - demands for a modern infrastructure, which usually has to be provided by the local community;
  - unrealistic assessment of the actual needs of a certain region.

o Advantages of enterprise zones from the entrepreneurs' perspective:
  - more rapid and less expensive construction of business premises; attraction of a strategic partner, which operates in the same location;
  - good working conditions and the possibility for personal development;
  - lower operating costs;
  - greater efficiency;
  - a quality support environment;
  - utilization of benefits, which the zone provides.

o Disadvantages of enterprise zones from the entrepreneurs' perspective:
  - the question of the ability to invest;
  - acceptance of rules which are in force within the zone.

Sweden

The basic objective of incubators – to give as many entrepreneurs as possible a chance to form a company of their own and make it grow, is in itself a paradox. There are limits to funding, and to available space. Therefore, the incubator can seldom offer support to as many entrepreneurs as it would like.

Some incubators provide too much support. We consider it to be important not to over-patronise the start-ups. They have to develop their own company and learn by their own mistakes. "There are no free lunches" so to speak. The purpose of the staff is to provide assistance and advice and to make the managers feel comfortable, not to do the manager's job.

We believe it is of great importance that we can offer the start-ups coming from the university an opportunity to work off of the university premises. It takes some companies much longer to be looked upon as real companies if they stay under the university umbrella while forming their company. "Just another university project" type of discussion is important to avoid.

The greatest strengths of an incubator are embodied in the interactivity of companies. The 'synergy' as some call it. Companies are generally encouraged to mix, share ideas, dreams, problems, and successes. Their energies feed one another. Their successes fuel competition and help to improve quality and speed development.

All the support given during the incubator phase shortens the total start-up time. The different investors have different goals. Shorter time to develop a product and shorter time to market means faster return on investments, increased company satisfaction, improved quality of life in a community through innovation, services, and jobs.the company and products/services.

Turkey

The benefits of an incubator include shared facilities and services provided at flexible and reasonable terms and rates, access to counselling and other resources, as well as increased credibility provided for the tenants. In more detailed terms, the advantages can be described as follows:
- o the incubator is nurturing diversified businesses, which is very important in an area where the whole economy is dependent on a dominant sector such as coal;
- o the cost of job creation in an incubator is

much below the average national figures. Considering that the benefits gained will accumulate year after year and additional jobs will be created, there is certainly an economic rationale for the public investment;
- o the presence of the incubator increases the value of surrounding property;
- o although the results are expected in the long run, there are clear signs that replication of the concept is being encouraged;

One of the issues that needs to be discussed is the role of subsidies as opposed to investment, including:
- o dependency relationship;
- o continuous need for cash infusion;
- o efforts for maintaining steady cash flow.

Ukraine

In adapting the best practices in United States incubators to Ukraine, some lessons learned include:

- o The "deep pockets" champion in the form of an economic development community has not yet been established in Ukraine. Knowing the importance of this best practice, the BID Programme was conceived. In this instance, Loyola College, with USAID funding support, serves as the "deep pockets" champion to provide the initial investment and ongoing business services. From the beginning, the development of sustainability was a management priority in structuring the programme. Both SBIs have been housed at institutes that have an interest in sustaining them because they provide (albeit small) revenue stream;

- o Where a minimal full-time staff, managing director and receptionist, was sufficient in the United States, it soon became clear that the incubators in Ukraine required more extensive staffing and organizational structure. This is due in part to the nature of doing business in Ukraine, the general business services that are available, and the inclusion of an integrated, intensive business education and training programme required for each of the client businesses. Both SBIs will operate as corporate spin-offs that allow them to accept income from clients. Short courses provided for in bulk to the STCU and the Kharkiv Marketing Assistance

Programme of USAID demonstrate the potential for sustained operations;

o It became soon apparent that small and medium-sized enterprises in the Ukraine were going to require extensive, formalized business training on the market-driven business model if they were to compete successfully. Consequently, a business education and training programme was developed that integrated business plan development as the entrepreneurs progressed through the course of study. On completion of this programme of study, each business owner has a completed business plan that is reviewed by a panel of experts. This evaluation is to provide feedback to the business owner of changes that need to be made in order to submit the business plan to a bank for loan acquisition. Perhaps even more importantly, the owner now has the business plan perspective and tools necessary to analyse business decisions to determine their profitability;

o ?Access to capital to sustain the Kiev SBI and Kharkiv SBI and to provide financial resources to the client firms for their sustained operations was not readily available. To meet this challenge, the USAID grant for the BID Programme contains funding for sustaining the incubators for the first two and a half years and funds for loan guarantees for the most qualified client companies. In essence, loans will be made to qualified borrowers through banking institutions in the form of loans guaranteed by the funds budgeted for loan guarantees in the USAID grant. The world-wide financial crisis that arrived in Ukraine in August 1998 delayed the implementation of the loan guarantee portion of the programme. In time, it is expected that the banking system in Ukraine will mature to the extent that the entrepreneurs will be able to acquire loans direct from the banks backed by agencies similar to the US Small Business Administration;

o ?The Kiev SBI and Kharkiv SBI incubators are located in the largest cities of Ukraine. While there is some participation in their training programmes by entrepreneurs from other regions, it was soon learned that extending the benefits to the rest of the country would require an explicit outreach

programme. Needs abound in Ukraine for business training for entrepreneurs located in the more remote portions of the country. Once the incubators in Kiev and Kharkiv are well established, they can begin a programme of outreach in a "hub and spoke" model. In this model, the hubs are Kiev and Kharkiv and the spokes are radials reaching out 100 to 200 kilometres to branch incubators or business information centres in smaller cities and towns where the municipal or oblast Government would provide some facilities and staff support;

o It has also become very clear that women and minorities represent a significant population of Ukraine's next generation of entrepreneurs and business owners. They represent a well-educated work force and are excellent candidates for technology-oriented businesses. Many are located in rural areas and are interested in starting micro enterprises. A proposal was recently submitted to the USAID micro enterprise programme that emphasizes support of women and the very poor, which could contribute to this outreach;

o Other cities in Ukraine are well positioned in terms of population, resources, and need for business training designed to help entrepreneurs grow their businesses and others who are interested in starting a new business to serve the needs of the community. After investigation, the two that appear to be the highest priority opportunities are Odessa and Dnipropetrovsk.

CHAPTER 8

FINANCE

Bulgaria

To take up serious positions in the high-tech sector, companies need to keep investing large funds in development and innovative activities. The most difficult problem to solve now in Bulgaria is financial support, currently under the rigid limitations of the Currency Board and the severe restrictions of the International Monetary Fund Agreement.

The Strategy and the draft law envisage that government support for funding high-tech activities is realized by: indirect support - by means of ceding tax and other resources and measures for attracting international support.

According to the draft law technology parks and their members need to pay a fixed percentage of the revenue gained from the activities, instead of the tax on the company profit. This has been determined by the features of the high-tech companies' long-term assets and the particular structure of their expenses, which are difficult to track and prove legal within the standard taxation framework.

The law also envisages that high technology parks set up funds, such as project funds to support technological and applied research and investment funds, to support the updating of the infrastructure and the construction of new sites in the parks. The money that goes to these funds has to be provided not less than a fixed percentage of the revenues after taxation, settled by the founders of the technology park.

Croatia

The list of institutions and their financial programmes for fostering SMEs in Croatia:

o   Programmes of the Croatian bank for reconstruction and development:
- credits for the investments in modernization and expansion of existing companies and crafts (up to 200 employees);
- credits for the Croatian citizens returning from Germany for founding companies and crafts;
- credits for establishing new companies and craft;
- credits for fostering small business in the war-devastated areas.

o   Programmes of commercial banks (Bjelovarska banka, Dalmatinska banka, Gospodarsko-kreditna banka, etc.):
- credits for further development of businesses;
- credits for establishing new companies.

o   Programmes of the Croatian guarantee agency:
- guarantees for small businesses (for credits up to DM 100,000);
- guarantees for small businesses in the war-devastated areas (for credits up to DM 100,000);
- programme of Development - guarantees for credits up to DM 350,000 for expanding successful private companies);
- programme of Start-up - guarantees for credits up to DM 100,000 for new small-sized companies or crafts which are using the services of the Croatian network of consultants.

o   Programmes of local Governments - cities, counties and municipalities that activate their own financial resources for credits with low interest rates.

o   The CARITAS - credit programme intended for small businesses ranging from DM 3,000 to 2,000.

Czech Republic

Supporting measures to SMEs are arranged mainly through institutions such as the Czech-Moravian Guarantee and Development Bank, the Agricultural and Forestry Fund, the Business Development Agency, regional advisory and information centres, business innovation centres (BICs), the Export Guarantee and Insurance Company, the Czech Export Bank, venture capital funds and others.

Finland

The promotion of business incubation has become an objective of the Government's SME policy. A body interested in starting business incubation activities can obtain aid from the Government's regional organization, the Centre for Employment and Economic Development, covering about half of the costs of a feasibility study. In addition, it has been possible to receive aid for the costs arising at the start-up stage of the operation. Further, aid may be granted for the consultation and training arranged by the incubator for start-ups.

Georgia

In order to provide services for incubators, financial resources are needed. Among the sources available in Georgia the following are the most prospective:
o   financing from central and local budgets;
o   international technical and economic assistance;
o   foreign loans;
o   voluntary contributions;
o   foreign investments.

Germany

The investment in an innovation centre (building, renovation, equipment) is provided mainly from public sources (municipalities and State programmes 50 - 90 percent). The other sources of investment finance are usually loans from the normal capital market.

The cost of operation in most cases was financially supported from public sources as well. The most common system is an annually decreasing amount of financial support with the aim of reaching self-financing three to five years after the opening of the innovation centre. Practice has shown that self financing (including servicing the initial investment) only can be reached in centres with a minimum of 3,000 - 5,000 m# of rental space.

Hungary

The following sources are available for creating and developing an industrial park:
o   entrepreneurial capital (domestic and foreign) can be used for the infrastructure of an industrial park. However, for SMEs the capital is needed rather for the essential internal infrastructure;
o   investment by local Governments: many local Governments possess land areas that can be used as a contribution in kind. They can also contribute through the construction of public utilities;
o   all counties have decentralized resources that they can use within their competence, e.g. to support infrastructure investments linked to industrial parks;
o   the Ministry of Economic Affairs has an agreement with the Ministry of Agriculture and Rural Development on the joint financing of the Industrial Park Programme. The funds are advertised jointly and a higher rate of subsidy is granted for industrial parks in a disadvantaged region.

The decisions on financing are made in a inter-ministerial council where all the above-mentioned institutions are represented.

Italy

These examples are based on business incubators in the south of Italy, which is an "Objective 1" area of the European Union. This means that there are a number of financing instruments in use including interest-free loans for activities, in some cases as much as 70% of the estimated investment, and employee training financed at 100%.

After start-up, the follow-up phase is financed with regional loans for quality certification, marketing projects and also for all the soft types of activity that require the hiring of external consultants.

Kyrgyzstan

Among the funds available for science parks and related institutions, the following are the most important:
o   loans and credits;
o   sponsor financing;
o   revenue from contracted services;
o   revenue from renting premises;
o   governmental resources assigned to the incubator.

Republic of Moldova

There is no financial aid from the Government or other donor institutions for any type of business incubator. However, the business incubator project envisages three stages of financing the activity:

- o Stage I: full financing from outside sources (founders, sponsors, donators) for a period of six months to one year as part of the initial package to start the activity of the incubator;
- o Stage II: partial outside financing for a period of one to one and a half years;
- o Stage III: self-financing after the initial II and I stage (estimated at one and a half to three years).

Russian Federation

Russian business incubators are funded from different sources. The funding can come from federal or regional budgets; municipal, city or regional employment centres; r
egional funds for SME support and development, from local businesses or from shareholders and sponsors.

In December 1997 a Seminar on the Problems, Results and Prospects for Business Incubators was held. According to the conclusions of the Seminar, the starting phase of a business incubator requires financing in the range of $160,000 to $ 1 million. A new incubator can attain the break-even level only within some years after its creation and even then only under favourable conditions. That is why the shareholders of the business incubator try to obtain funding from different sources, such as federal, regional and municipal budgets, and from regional SME support funds.

Efforts are made to attract funding from industrial enterprises, banks, institutions and universities. In some cases funding can be provided by foreign partners through grants, donations, etc. Support and assistance from organizations and individuals may be not only financial resources but also in kind, such as space, equipment, training, services to the incubated SMEs and entrepreneurs.

Sweden

Most of the Swedish incubators are financed with public local and regional funds, but there is also a national programme financed by the Swedish National Board for Industrial and Technical Development and money from the national employment agencies in the regions.

Private funding is also used in some incubators and private incubator initiatives are becoming increasingly common.

Turkey

KOSGEB allocates the funds necessary to establish and operate an incubator. These funds are available for refurbishment, office equipment and furnishings as well as operating expenses, with a decreasing rate of cost reimbursement for a period of three to four years. A business plan needs to be prepared with a view to attaining self-sustainability with the following elements:

- o the key characteristics of the region;
- o a mission statement;
- o the objectives;
- o a management model;
- o an action plan;
- o a financial forecast for five years;
- o a contemplated contribution to costs.

Payments will then be made by KOSGEB on a cost-reimbursement basis, and the incubator is also entitled to advance payment. All the transactions and expenditures of the incubator are audited by both KOSGEB and independent auditors in accordance with the generally accepted standards.

CHAPTER 9

CUSTOMERS

Bulgaria

Incubators can develop various criteria to select their potential clients, to work in a group of sectors of industry or to concentrate in a certain product niche. Given the status of Bulgarian SMEs, one of the major criteria of efficiency of a high technology park during the forthcoming years will be the increase in the number of companies successfully operating in the park, financially viable and fully independent when they leave the incubators.

Members and clients of the park can be small and medium-sized high-tech companies at the stage of development and, as well as bigger high-tech companies seeking suitable infrastructure, intellectual environment and cooperation with SMEs.

Croatia

A potential entrepreneur can become a tenant of a business incubator only upon the completion of a selection process, which begins with interviews with the applicants, aimed at assessing the viability of the business ideas. Preference is given to applicants, who have programmes that are of interest for the development This is followed by the formulation of a business plan. The programmes that are assessed positively can enter the incubator, i.e. its originator becomes a tenant of the incubator.

As an example, the criteria for entering the Porin centre include:
o Technological novelty and market potential of the firm's product
o Potential profitability of the tenant firm and its flexibility I the face of market disturbances
o The firm's potential to create jobs
o Hiring of premises of up to 50 m²

Czech Republic

The different business incubators have very different customer profiles. Tenant companies come from different fields such as environment,

chemistry, physics, information technology, material science, biotechnology and medicine.

Estonia

The Incubation Centre in Tartu was set up in 1993. After the launching period the number of tenant companies has stabilized to around 25 - mainly due to the limited capacity of premises. The tenant companies are chosen through a system of open tenders by the General Board, based on their accordance with the goals and after expert evaluation of their business plans. Start-up companies or projects accepted for incubation will consequently enjoy certain concessions such as partially credited rents and services. The overall turnover of the tenant companies has increased almost tenfold during the last four years.

A serious problem for an incubator is the low motivation of people to start up a business. This is caused by:
o a lack of start up capital (hard to obtain it for "beginners");
o a lack of business experience (information management and marketing);
o problems in finding a proper place and premises for starting the business (a large amount of start-up funds is spent on offices and office equipment instead of using it as working capital).

The aim of incubation is to utilize the experience and skills of partner institutions via their contribution to these project activities that are mostly related to:

o creating a favourable environment for small businesses;
o increasing the number of newly established enterprises, and jobs; improving the competitiveness of SMEs and the skills of management and employees;
o promoting product and technological development and technology transfer;
o disseminating information on new technologies, current domestic and foreign innovation projects, offers and demands for partnership;
o preparing adequate project proposals and properly completing project applications.

The first steps in the creation of an incubator include a business plan, the preparation of premises for 12 - 15 companies, the recruitment and education of staff, as well as the development of business development advisory and mentoring programmes.

Finland

The success of a business incubator depends to a great extent on the choice of tenant. A precondition for a successful choice is a suitable location and a favourable environment where there are potential tenants, among which the selection can be made. Another precondition is that the incubator has a clear business idea and strategy on which the selection of the tenants is based. Thirdly, the selection criteria corresponding to the business idea and the strategy are necessary for the practical choice of tenants.

In a recent survey, it was found out that two thirds of Finnish business incubators consider the following criteria as indispensable:
   o   the entrepreneur is credible as person;
   o   the enterprise fits into the business idea of the incubator;
   o   there are customers and a market for the products of the enterprise
   o   other crucial criteria include a ralistic budget, growth potential, the age of the firm (may not exceed three years), an existing business plan, competitive technology and ability to pay the rent.

The business incubator and the tenant usually sign a contract. It contains the rules of thegame, the services to be provided by the incubator, development measures to be taken by the entrepreneur and the payment due to the incubator during the period of incubation when a business idea is to be transformed into a successful business. The agreement may also be extended to thetime following the actual incubation period.

A precondition for tenants approved for incubation is that they must be at the initial stage in their operations, normally not older than three years. They are assumed to stay in the incubation for a few years and then to move to other premises.

At a seminar on business incubation that Finland organized in cooperation with the European Commission in 1998, the importance of a suitable mix of new and existing enterprises in incubation was emphasized. This is important for both parties as it offers a mutual opportunity to learn. It also contributes to inreased confidence of the customers in the operation of the incubator. As for technology enterprises, the cooperation between enterprises in incubation and other firms of the same type is promoted by the fact that business incubators linked to a university form part of a science park or technology centre within an area where even other technology-oriented enterprises are located.

Germany

As there are numerous types of innovation centre in Germany (technology/knowledge-based, mixed use, no-tech etc.) it is not possible to give a general description of tenants/customers. In technology oriented innovation centres a large portion of customers are (start-up) enterprises with a research/university background. In "non-tech" innovation centres the focus is more on the local business potential.

Innovation centres usually "generate" their customers from local resources. There are only a few examples where tenants have been acquired over long geographical distances. Such cases, for instance, are to be found where specific technology potentials and/ or concentrations are to be

found and needed by the specific individual entrepreneur. However, the typical case is the start-up entrepreneur from the same city or region.

In recent years innovation centres in Germany began to serve customers (companies) that were not tenants of the centres. The regional business network is thus developing and its synergy potential is increasing. Examples of such services are technology transfer (access to know-how from research facilities), joint product development projects or marketing activities (e.g. national, international fair participation).

Hungary

In Hungary there are many types of business incubator with local features. In general, however, they all provide small new enterprises lacking capital with a chance to grow. At the time of moving into the incubator the enterprise must not have exceeded the age of three years and it an stay in the incubator for a maximum of four to five years. For the sake of sustainable operation there are no sectoral restrictions, but innovative, potentially growing small enterprises and those that increase employment are given priority. Priority is given to certain industries such as enterprises in the production industries, companies providing services for other companies (for example those residing in the incubator house) and other service companies. The least promoted branch is trade.

Kyrgyzstan

Clients of an incubator can be divided into two groups:
- o enterprises that are being incubated - that is the tenants who have access to the basic and extended services;
- o external companies that the incubator attracts in the region. This group can consist of enterprises that need additional information and access to some of the services.

Republic of Moldova

Clients and members of business incubators can be any enterprises registered as a subject of entrepreneurship of the Republic of Moldova.

Russian Federation

The profile of business incubator customers in Russia usually reflects the specifics of the regions. Client policy, which describes the selection criteria, is usually stated in the basic documents of a business incubator. For instance, business incubators oriented for job creation for the retired service men must first of all solve this social problem. There are incubators designed primarily to help provide jobs for women, which give priorities to the enterprises with a high number of women employed.

Often the profile of the tenants by specialization is being dictated by the structure of local economy. Only start-ups that meet current local needs can successfully operate in the region.

Most of the business incubators try to attract small businesses with innovative technologies that have high potential to compete in the market.

Many incubators declare up-front certain kinds of business activity that they do not provide support for.

Slovenia

Innovative and technology developmental companies need to have an appropriate balance sheet and a business plan. The services to the companies are subsidized by the Ministry of Science and Technology. The maximum duration of membership is five years.

The business programmes offered to the tenants include:
- o environmental protection technologies;
- o computer and information technologies;
- o regional industry such as mechanical engineering, chemical industry and others included in the Phare Cross-Border Cooperation Programme.

Sweden

The target groups for the incubator programmes are:
- o students and researchers at universities with an entrepreneurial spirit and a business idea;
- o entrepreneurial employees at existing knowledge-intensive companies that want to spin-off with a business opportunity or just to start-up a new venture;
- o others with entrepreneurial spirit and a strong business concept.

The basic idea is that it is better to offer too many possibilities to test than not to try at all. Finally, it is the market that will be the judge.

CHAPTER 10

LEGAL STATUS AND REGULATORY LEGISLATION

In addition to providing the legal framework mentioned above, Governments should recognize that all forms of local business advisory centres can play a vital role in economic development and should encourage the creation of such centres in areas where local institutions are prepared to nurture them.

National Governments should work with local Governments, universities, and other local entities to identify locations, create advisory centres, train their staff, and support them financially for a sufficient period of time to make them sustainable. National Governments can also help by providing resources for training, capital for client companies, tax and regulatory relief for clients, etc.

Bulgaria

The strategy and the drafted law on high technology activity and high technology parks form the legal framework, within which the official relations are settled, and sets the conditions for the development of high technology activities through the high technology parks. The draft law:
- o regulates the management at government level as well as the role of the individual institutions including the Council of Ministers, the Ministry of Economy, the Ministry of Education and Science as well as the Bulgarian Academy of Sciences and others;
- o provides the legal basis for the support of high technology activities and parks;
- o establishes the requirements and the terms for the creation and registration of technoparks by the competent government authorities in the country.

High technology parks and the companies operating in the parks shall be registered in order to guarantee the targeted use of the privileges provided.

Some amendments in other legal acts are also envisaged in order to remove barriers to innovation and technology development.

Croatia

There is no legal definition of a business incubator, technology centre or a science park in Croatia. The National Science and Research Programme defines the National network of technology centres, which serves as the official framework for establishing incubators for technology based enterprises.

The legal framework important for registration and operation of the technoparks includes common civil laws such as:
- o Law on Commercial Companies;
- o Law on Obligations;
- o Law on Labour;
- o Law on Free Zones;
- o Law on Industrial Property;
- o Trade Law;
- o Accounting Law.

Czech Republic

There are a number of legislative acts covering issues related to business incubation in the Czech Republic:
- o Commercial Code (Act No. 513/1991 Coll., effective from 1 January 1992, amended in 1992 and 1993);
- o Trade Licensing Act (also known as Small Business Act No. 455/1991 Coll., in force from 1 January 1992, several times amended);
- o Czech National Council Act No. 299/1992 Coll., State Support to Small and Medium-Sized Enterprises;
- o Act No. 272/1996 Coll.

Georgia

Georgia's legislative framework is based on internationally adopted principles and norms The most important market economy oriented documents are the Civil Code, the Tax Code, and the law on Entrepreneurship as well as the law on the Promotion and Guarantees of Investment Activities, and the law on Small Business Protection, which define the basic norms.

Germany

German innovation centres are fully integrated

in the "normal" legal structure. This means that there is no specific law or regulation governing the activities of the centres. The most common, almost exclusive, legal form is "GmbH" (company with limited liability). As far as public finance is provided for investments and/or operation cost, the applicable budget regulations have to be respected as well.

The Association of German Innovation Centres (ADT) is an independent organization run exclusively by its members. ADT does not have financial support from public sources. The Association was established by its members to develop expertise and improve the exchange of experience between the innovation centres and to promote their interest in the public.

Hungary

There are no direct regulations on the operation of incubators. The Government Decree on the medium-term strategy of SME development mentions incubators as a means of SME development.

The legal background of the industrial park programme were created by:
- o the law on Regional Development;
- o the Government Decree on Industrial Parks;
- o the Decree of the Ministry of Industry, Trade and Tourism on the operation of the application system of Industrial Parks.

Industrial parks can be very different and, thus, the objective is to provide as many possibilities for SMEs as possible. Industrial parks can provide innovation and technological services, which makes it practical to settle near universities and research institutions. They can provide logistical and technological transfer services as well. However, all of them should operate as an incubator.

To establish an industrial park in Hungary, the following criteria need to be met:
- o the candidate should possess a minimum of 10 hectares of land area. Smaller plots are not suitable for launching such activity. Candidates who could present further alternatives for enlargement are preferred;
- o the candidate should possess the title of ownership of the property or a long-term lease. This criterion is indispensable for sustainable long-term financing or state subsidising;

- o the realization of the planned industrial park should be included in the development strategy of the county. It guarantees the long-term survival as well;
- o the candidate should prepare a feasibility study, a business plan and a marketing strategy, without which the effectiveness of investment and support is not measurable.

Kyrgyzstan

The business incubators in Kyrgyzstan can be non-governmental organizations, public foundations or private companies. The legislation regulating the juridical status of such activities includes different private-enterprise related laws, such as the Civil Code, the Bill on State Registration and the Government Decree on the Basic Scheme for the Classification of Enterprise Types. There are no laws or government decrees regulating the operations of business incubators per se.

Latvia

Based on the above-mentioned concept the first technology-oriented business-support structures were established in 1993. Today, there are three innovative business-support institutions in Latvia:
- o The Latvian Technological Centre (1993);
- o The Latvian Technology Park at the Riga Technical University (1996);
- o The Latvian Electronic Industry Business Innovation Centre (1997).

All these structures are non-profit limited liability companies initiated and financed by public organizations (ministries, municipalities). The main criterion for their establishment is a business plan or a concept approved by the founders.

Republic of Moldova

The regulating framework in the Republic of Moldova includes:
- o the Fiscal Code;
- o the Government Programme on the Support and Development of SMEs;
- o the law on the Support and Protection of Small Business.

There is a need to adopt a Government Decree on Business Incubators and accompanying regulatory acts.

Contents